A Brief History of Asia's Sustained Growth

This book explores Asia's remarkable economic transformation by examining four key nations—Japan, Korea, China and India. It presents how these countries sustained high economic growth, leading to prosperity.

This book analyses the four economies through the four pillars: (a) free and open markets, (b) accountable government and effective policies, (c) education and human capital development and (d) saving and investment, leading to capital accumulation. The analysis reveals that the experiences of the four countries are highly divergent. Against common knowledge that the Asian miracle was based on export-driven, government-led and infrastructure investment strategy, these countries achieved high economic growth by building the four pillars of their own which reflected their history, culture and initial economic situation. Noting that the present global economic environment makes a copy-and-paste tactic impossible for developing economies to follow, this book offers broader insights on institutional reform and the timely exploitation of critical opportunities, which will be of interest to other developing nations.

Written by an experienced economist and policymaker, this concise book will appeal to students and researchers of development economics, political economy and Asian studies. It will also appeal to general readers interested in learning more about global economics and history.

In-chang SONG obtained his PhD in Economics from the University of York, UK. An economist and policymaker, he has more than three decades of experience in international economic cooperation, financial policy and development strategy in the Korean Ministry of Finance and MDBs. He was Deputy Minister and G20 Sherpa for the Republic of Korea.

Routledge Studies in Development Economics

205 Artificial Intelligence and SMEs in Developing Economies
Edited by Timilehin Olasoji Olubiyi and Tulus T.H. Tambunan

206 Public Debt in Kenya
An Economic History
Aaron Thegeya

207 Ethical Economics and Sustainable Development
The Role of Moral Capital
Edited by Devi Datt Tewari and Kehinde Damilola Ilesanmi

208 Sustainable Development in Southern Africa
The Critical Role of Public Governance
Edited by Tonderai Kapesa and Nirmala Dorasamy

209 The Impact of Microfinance
Poverty Reduction and Financial Inclusion in the Global South
Agnes Olatokunbo Martins

210 African Economic Development
Myths, Models and Policies
Beryl Adongo Oranga and Robert Buckley

211 A Brief History of Asia's Sustained Growth
Japan, Korea, China, and India's Economic Transformation
In-Chang SONG

For more information about this series, please visit: www.routledge.com/Routledge-Studies-in-Development-Economics/book-series/SE0266

A Brief History of Asia's Sustained Growth

Japan, Korea, China and India's Economic Transformation

In-chang SONG

Routledge
Taylor & Francis Group
LONDON AND NEW YORK

First published 2026
by Routledge
4 Park Square, Milton Park, Abingdon, Oxon OX14 4RN

and by Routledge
605 Third Avenue, New York, NY 10158

Routledge is an imprint of the Taylor & Francis Group, an informa business

British Library Cataloguing-in-Publication Data
A catalogue record for this book is available from the British Library

ISBN: 9781041353126 (hbk)
ISBN: 9781041353164 (pbk)
ISBN: 9781003797135 (ebk)

DOI: 10.4324/9781003797135

Typeset in Times New Roman
by codeMantra

Contents

Preface

Economics 101 teaches that growth arises from two sources: technological progress and increases in productive factors such as labor and capital. In my 20s and 30s, I took this proposition for granted and assumed that growth was an almost automatic process available to all countries. After more than three decades working on development across Asia and other continents, I have reached a very different conclusion. The pathways to growth and prosperity vary widely across countries. Unfortunately, many countries and their people have hardly benefited from economic growth and prosperity.

In Asia, Japan took flight first, followed by Korea, China and India, much like a flock of geese in formation. Why do geese fly in a formation of V? By flying together, they can travel substantially faster and longer, often cited as up to about 70% farther than flying alone. The lead bird's wingbeats create an aerodynamic upwash that reduces air resistance for those behind. Development economist *Kiyoshi Kojima*, in his theory of 'flying geese paradigm', cast Japan as the lead economy whose industrial upgrading and technology diffusion paved the way for later industrializers in the region. I disagree with this interpretation because Japan did not unilaterally confer benefits on other Asian economies throughout the region's development.

Over the long journey of economic growth, Asian economies have rotated leadership and followership. Leaders have sometimes ceded position to recover, while others took the front, allowing countries to exchange advantages along the path to prosperity. Today, Japan, Korea, China, ASEAN and India are tightly linked through global value chains, benefiting one another by supplying markets, technology, raw materials, parts and intermediate goods.

The objective of this book is to examine the core drivers of economic success in Japan, Korea, China and India (hereafter, the *Four Asian Geese*). Economists and policymakers have long sought to identify the common elements behind their growth and to distill lessons for neighbors still striving to escape poverty. Yet many Asian countries have not yet stepped onto the ladder of sustained growth, and others that once gained a foothold have stalled before climbing further. In all such cases, this book aims to serve as a practical reference for charting a path toward lasting prosperity.

I admit that there is no single silver bullet that enables every country to overcome its obstacles in achieving economic growth. Geography, population size, land and resource endowments and political institutions differ widely and create distinct challenges. Whereas the Four Asian Geese are large in territory and population, smaller economies—for example, island countries in the Pacific—confront problems that the Four Asian Geese have never experienced. Accordingly, the conclusions and lessons presented here should not be read as a universal playbook. Rather, they can serve as reference points that developing countries may consult when charting a route for growth.

The experiences of the Four Asian Geese are highly divergent. They differ across a wide range of dimensions. Over millennia, they have followed distinct historical trajectories. They vary in geography, climate, resource endowments, language, culture and religion. While each country's success may offer specific lessons, their stories, considered together and in comparison, can yield sharper and deeper insights. My hope is that this book helps other developing countries embark on the path to prosperity and succeed in improving the lives of many.

At the same time, and equally importantly, the Four Asian Geese are now confronting slower growth. Japan has struggled for three decades since the early 1990s' burst of asset prices. Korea's potential growth rate has fallen below 2%. China can no longer sustain 8%–10% annual expansion amid an adverse global environment. India still has a considerable distance to travel before converging with advanced economies. In this sense, this book can be useful not only for other developing countries but also for the Four Asian Geese themselves.

To overcome present challenges and shape a more prosperous future, the Four Asian Geese must first understand the sources of their past success accurately. Misreading history will hinder effective responses to today's economic headwinds. Past policy prescriptions such as targeted industrial policy, export-led strategies and massive infrastructure investments work no longer under the changed circumstances. This book seeks to find alternative ways, which can help the Four Asian Geese continue to fly both faster and farther in the future.

1 Asia's Journey for Economic Growth

1.1 Story of Four Asian Geese' flight

1.1.1 Flying faster and farther

In 1961, Japanese economist *Kaname Akamatsu* published a paper titled "A Theory of Unbalanced Growth in the World Economy". He examined economic experiences of countries and identified a pattern of sequential growth. He observed that production in certain industries shifted from a leading country to a following one. The leader would then move into industries with higher value-added production, while the follower would take over the industry left behind. Less developed economies first engaged in low-wage production, but as their costs increased, they transferred such production to countries at an earlier stage of development. Through this process, both the leader and the follower benefited.

The growth pattern of Asian economies after World War II resembled a formation of flying geese. Japan took the lead, followed by Korea, Taiwan, Singapore and Hong Kong. Later, China, ASEAN countries and India joined this sequence. The apparel industry is a good example of this pattern. Ship building and automobile manufacturing also followed the same sequence. In some cases, entire industries relocated to less developed countries. However, in most sectors, advanced economies focused on high-technology production and transferred labor-intensive production to less developed ones. This process formed what looked like a flying-geese pattern of industrial development.

Today, Asia's economic structure has, however, changed greatly. There is no single leading country across all industries. Japan remains strong in precision machinery and chemicals. Korea leads in semiconductors and shipbuilding. China has become a leader in electric vehicles and battery. Asian economies now function more like a network than a simple flying-geese formation. Japan, Korea, China, India and ASEAN countries are closely connected through global value chains. They support each other by providing broader markets and advanced technology. FDIs and financial investment are flowing across the borders in both directions.

DOI: 10.4324/9781003797135-1

This complex web of interconnection shows that economic development no longer follows a single or predictable pattern. The growth of a country does not necessarily progress from labor-intensive and low-technology industries to capital-intensive and high-technology ones. As a result, the historical experience of one country cannot be directly applied to another. What is more meaningful is to identify the common factors that have supported economic growth across different economies in the region.

The starting point of this book is the idea that many Asian economies share certain characteristics that have driven their economic success. These shared features have allowed them to grow more rapidly and to sustain higher growth over time. In this context, I refer to Japan, Korea, China and India as the 'Four Asian Geese'. The next section will explain why these four countries were selected for analysis.

1.1.2 Why these four countries?

During 1960–2018, developing Asia's[1] per capita GDP grew at an impressive average annual rate of 4.7%. This was the fastest among all world regions and a record in modern economic history. However, growth performance differed greatly across subregions. East Asia achieved the highest rate at about 6.5%, led by China at 6.8%. In contrast, the Pacific and Central Asia expanded slowly, at around 1.5% and 2.0%, respectively. South Asia and Southeast Asia fell between these extremes, showing moderate but steady growth.[2]

In this book, I focus on four countries—Japan, Korea, China and India—because each represents a broader group of economies in the region at a comparable stage of development. Japan was the first Asian country to reach the income level of advanced economies. Korea, Taiwan, Singapore and Hong Kong formed, following Japan, a group of high-performing economies known as the 'Four Asian Tigers'. Among these, Hong Kong and Singapore are city-states, and Taiwan is less exposed to global trade. Korea stands out for its scale and deep integration into global value chains.

The next group includes the ASEAN economies, along with China, and then India and other latecomers. Selecting China and India as representatives from these groups is natural given their population size, economic weight and growing influence in the global economy.[3] While ASEAN countries are expanding rapidly, their development paths are too diverse to be analyzed comprehensively within this book's scope.

The discussion here does not aim to provide a full economic history of the four countries. Instead, it focuses on their periods of take-off and rapid economic expansion of 30–40 years. The analysis also considers a few years before the take-off periods to capture the broader transition.

Japan, despite heavy wartime destruction, recovered quickly and achieved more than two decades of strong growth from the early 1950s, returning to the ranks of advanced economies in the 1980s. Korea's take-off came later due to the devastation of the Korean War (1950–1953). From the early 1960s it grew rapidly through export-oriented industrialization. China began its shift toward a market economy after the 1978 reforms, sustaining remarkable growth for more than 40 years. India launched major economic reforms in 1991, reducing state control and opening to trade and foreign investment, which led to accelerated growth as market forces gained strength.

1.2 Four pillars for higher economic growth

Before the Industrial Revolution in the mid-1700s, there was little difference between rich and poor countries and individuals. Most people lived in poverty, except for a small number of royal families and privileged elites. Around that time, however, two remarkable changes began to reshape the world.

First, the global population began to rise sharply. In the first century, the world's population was about 230 million. By 1800, it had grown to around 900 million, but between 1800 and 2000 it increased sixfold. The rapid growth of population was largely the result of major advances in agriculture, medicine and public health. The Agricultural Revolution, followed by the Industrial Revolution, increased food production and improved transportation and sanitation, reducing famine and disease. As death rates declined and life expectancy rose, the global population expanded at an unprecedented pace.

Second, income per person, which had remained nearly stagnant during 1500–1800, increasing by only about 50%, rose ninefold in 1800–2000. This dramatic rise in income was driven by industrialization, technological innovation and the expansion of global trade. Mechanization and the use of new energy sources, such as coal and later electricity, made mass production possible and greatly improved efficiency. At the same time, expanding global markets and advances in communication and transportation allowed countries to specialize in production and trade more effectively. These changes created unprecedented economic growth and lifted millions of people out of poverty.

The Industrial Revolution introduced a wave of technological breakthroughs, including steam engines, electricity and major advances in transportation. These innovations suggested that technology could be shared and thus poor countries could eventually benefit from their spread. However, the history of the past 200 years tells a more complex story. The benefits of industrialization and technological progress were not equally distributed.

Over the past 70 years, Asia has experienced an economic transformation of historic scale. In 1960, Asia's per capita GDP was only $330. By 2018, it had risen to $4,903, an increase of nearly 15 times. During the same period, global per capita GDP merely tripled. As a result, Asia's share of global GDP expanded from 4% to 24%. The transformation was extraordinary not only in quantity but also in quality. An agrarian, low-income Asia of the 1960s evolved into a global manufacturing hub, marked by innovation, urbanization and a growing middle class. Life expectancy rose, infant mortality fell and education levels improved dramatically across the region.

The 'Four Asian Geese', Japan, Korea, China and India, led this transformation. Japan began its modern economic growth, overcoming the defeat in the World War II, and achieved high economic growth in the 1950s and 1960s. Korea, along with Taiwan, Singapore and Hong Kong, followed Japan in the 1960s and the 1970s and grew even faster than Japan. In the 1990s, several Southeast Asian countries and China joined the wave of economic growth. Now, India is closing the gap with its Asian peers. While it may be difficult to define a single 'Asian model' of economic growth, there are clear common factors—what I call 'common genes'—that helped these four economies sustain high and long-lasting growth.

There are many ways to understand the common genes behind the success of the Four Asian Geese. As the saying goes, success has many fathers. In this book, I focus on the most crucial factors that supported their long-term growth. These factors can be classified into four pillars:

1 Free and open market economy,
2 Accountable government and effective policies,
3 Education and human resource development, and
4 High savings and investment, leading to capital accumulation.

In the next sections, I will explore how each of these pillars generally helped economies take off, maintain momentum and achieve sustained prosperity over the long run.

1.2.1 Free and open market economy

Every economy must answer three basic questions: what to produce, how to produce and who will receive the products. In a non-market economy, these decisions are made by governments or elite groups, whereas, in a market economy, the answers emerge through the functioning of the market. More precisely, the market does not provide the answers directly. Market provides institutional arrangements that enable individuals and firms to discover them. The key players in this process are entrepreneurs, motivated by profit and committed to success through persistent and vigorous competition.

Entrepreneurs take risks while navigating uncertainty. When they make poor decisions, they lose money and become poorer. When they make wise choices, they earn profits and grow wealthier. This simple dynamic motivates them to work diligently, use resources efficiently and enhance productivity. Because individuals are free to compete, the overall economy becomes more dynamic, productive and faster growing. In contrast, a socialist system diminishes personal motivation to excel by restricting individual choice and removing the incentive of profit.

In this book, a 'free and open market system' means two key things: private ownership and economic freedom. Private ownership can exist only when laws and social order protect property rights. Adam Smith, a leading advocate of the market economy, emphasized that governments should provide defense, justice, infrastructure, education and healthcare. These essential functions form the foundation of a sound and sustainable market system.

Economic freedom is often seen as *laissez-faire*, meaning less government intervention. The so-called 'Washington Consensus'[4] is typical. It promotes free trade, open markets, fiscal discipline, privatization and minimal government intervention. However, when countries such as the US and Germany were industrializing, they relied heavily on state intervention and protectionist policies.[5] They used high tariffs to protect infant industries, provided government subsidies, invested in infrastructure and education and often restricted foreign competition to support domestic growth mainly against British products.

For developing countries, openness lies at the core of economic policy aimed at achieving rapid growth. Opening to global competition pushes firms to innovate and improve productivity. Trade liberalization increases efficiency because only the most competitive companies survive. Just as a country cannot nurture world-class football players without joining the World Cup, it cannot build world-class industries without competing globally.[6] The biggest advantage of openness lies in competition. Openness with economic freedom brings competition, and competition drives progress. Open trade and foreign investment boost efficiency, spread new technologies, and create long-term growth. Greater openness allows countries to learn, innovate and achieve economies of scale.

The idea that a domestic market should be protected in the early stage of economic development has long been debated among economists and policymakers. It is often associated with the argument about infant industry, which suggests that new industries need temporary protection until they become competitive. However, while this approach has potential benefits, it also carries significant drawbacks. On the positive side, protecting domestic industries can help young firms grow and gain competitiveness. On the negative side, prolonged protection often leads to inefficiency. Once industries are shielded from international competition, they may lose incentives to innovate or reduce costs. Therefore, protection must be carefully designed, time-bound and accompanied by clear performance goals. A successful policy strikes a balance between short-term protection and long-term competitiveness.

1.2.2 Accountable government and effective policies

In his 1968 book, "Asian Drama: An Inquiry into the Poverty of Nations", Swedish economist *Gunnar Myrdal* described much of developing Asia as being in the 'doldrums'. He argued that the region was trapped by governments' inability to design and implement effective development policies while facing rapid population growth. Decades later, *Daron Acemoglu* and *James Robinson*, in their influential book, "Why Nations Fail", offered a sharper view by writing "Poor countries are poor because those who hold power make choices that create poverty. They get it wrong not by mistake or ignorance but on purpose". Their point highlights how deeply politics shape economic progress. Political systems determine who leads, who governs and ultimately what policies are implemented.

History shows that prosperous nations have governments that are accountable, responsive and effective in creating conditions for growth. Acemoglu and Robinson explain that 'inclusive' political and economic institutions promote prosperity, while 'extractive' institutions lead to stagnation and poverty. Inclusive institutions encourage individuals to use their skills and talents freely and to make choices that benefit both themselves and society. In contrast, extractive institutions are designed to transfer wealth and power from one group to another, concentrating benefits among elites.

This raises an important question: does democracy support economic growth? Or, more directly, is democracy essential for it? The relationship between democracy and economic growth has long been debated. A political system is a framework for distributing resources and resolving conflicts. Democracy executes this function through majority rule. Economist Robert Barro once claimed that the overall effect of democracy on growth is weakly negative. He claimed that democracy might encourage growth when political freedoms are limited but could restrain it once a moderate level of freedom is achieved. Because majority voting often reflects the interests of established groups, democracy can sometimes slow down reforms needed for long-term growth.

History shows that authoritarian regimes can either foster or hinder growth. On the one hand, they can avoid some of democracy's weaknesses, such as political instability and slow decision-making. They implement large-scale reforms without political opposition, leading to economic growth. On the other, they risk turning into extractive systems where those in power enrich themselves instead of serving the public. The lack of accountability and potential for corruption or policy mistakes can lead to inefficiency and stagnation.

Most developed countries began their economic journeys with limited political rights and reached full democracy only after achieving higher income levels. In contrast, many newly independent Asian nations after World War II adopted democratic systems before establishing strong state capacity. As a result, they often struggled to maintain law and order or provide basic public goods. Several postwar democracies faced political instability and lacked strategic direction, which slowed their economic growth.

Korean economist and policymaker *Cho Yunjae* once noted, "To successfully implement credit policies and promote industrialization and growth, government commitment must be firm and visible, supported by strong political leadership". Indeed, Asia's economic success depended heavily on effective policies and strong institutions. A key question remains: why did some Asian governments succeed while others failed, despite following similar economic policies? The answer lied in leadership quality and bureaucratic competence, which largely determined whether policies were effectively implemented or not.

Governments play several fundamental roles in promoting economic growth. They provide infrastructure such as energy, transportation, water systems, telecommunications and information networks, which are public goods essential for development. Accountable governments ensure that these are efficiently built and maintained. Another critical role is ensuring macroeconomic stability through sound fiscal management, stable financial systems, low inflation and job creation. These elements are vital for sustainable growth and for avoiding crises.

However, this book does not examine infrastructure provision or macroeconomic management in detail. These areas vary widely across countries and require context-specific analysis. Many developing nations have built large and sophisticated infrastructure projects, such as dams, roads, bridges and ports, only to find themselves burdened with heavy debt. Instead, the focus will be on how the quality of governance, leadership and institutional design has shaped the success and failure of economic development across the Four Asian Geese.

1.2.3 Education and human resource development

It is widely acknowledged that investment in human capital through education and training increases employment, productivity and income growth. For this reason, economists generally agree that education and human capital provide an essential foundation for economic growth.[7] A large body of empirical research also supports this view, showing a significant relationship between the level and quality of education and long-term economic performance.

However, some studies questioned the strength of this relationship. They found no consistent correlation between average years of schooling[8] and the rate of economic growth across countries. One possible explanation is that educated individuals sometimes use their skills for rent-seeking or unproductive activities rather than for improving productivity. As a result, statistical analyses have not always confirmed that longer schooling directly leads to faster economic growth.[9]

This, however, should not be interpreted as meaning that education is irrelevant to growth. Education played a decisive role in economic take-off and sustained growth. It equips people with the capacity to absorb advanced technologies from developed countries. The benefits of trade openness and foreign investment can be realized only when citizens have the knowledge and skills to take advantage of them. Without an educated population, openness can lead to dependency on external forces rather than self-sustained growth. As human capital improved, technological progress accelerated, which in turn created greater demand for skilled workers, forming a virtuous cycle between education, technology and growth.

Beyond providing skilled labor, education also supports political stability and accountable governance.[10] Education empowers individuals to think critically, act independently and reject harmful traditions. It strengthens ethical standards and civic responsibility, which are necessary for a stable and productive society. Therefore, accumulation of human capital through education alone does not capture its full contribution to national development.[11]

It is important to note how education turns large population into productive human capital. Economists have long debated whether large population promotes or hinders economic progress. Evidence supports all three possibilities:[12] restriction, promotion or neutrality. The key determinant is how a country can best use affluent population to support development. Many low-income countries failed to do so because overpopulation hindered growth by reducing savings and slowing capital accumulation. Education was the factor that transformed population growth from a burden into a driver of development.[13]

1.2.4 Savings and investment, leading to capital accumulation

Economists generally agree, though with some differences in emphasis, that economic growth is driven mainly by capital accumulation through savings and investment, along with technological progress. In this regard, developing countries face two major challenges in achieving growth through capital accumulation in the early stages of development. First, their domestic savings are typically very low because most income is spent on basic consumption. Second, their financial systems are often weak and unable to effectively mobilize and allocate savings into productive investments.

Domestic savings in an economy are generated by households, businesses and governments. In early stages, agriculture-based economies, household savings play a crucial role. Yet low-income households tend to spend almost all their income on necessities, leaving little or nothing to save. In extreme cases, they even borrow or deplete existing assets, consuming what could have been saved for the future. This inability to save or invest in human and physical capital traps families and entire countries in a cycle of poverty known as 'the poverty trap'.

With economic development, the share of agriculture in total output and employment declines. This might suggest that agriculture becomes less important, but in fact, a productive agricultural sector is critical for economic take-off in the early stages of development. Agriculture provides food security, generates surplus income for savings, supplies raw materials for industry and creates demand for manufactured goods and services. Historical evidence suggests that most countries have achieved successful industrialization only after developing a strong agricultural base. A dynamic rural economy has therefore often served as an important steppingstone for reducing poverty and initiating sustained economic growth.

In this book, I emphasize the importance of agriculture in generating domestic savings before industrialization.[14] In the Four Asian Geese, land reforms[15] served as a turning point, though its form varied across countries. Land reform increased rural income and strengthened incentives for farmers to work harder and invest more in their land and farming tools. By giving ownership rights to small farmers, it encouraged savings and productivity growth. This, in turn, helped create the foundation for industrial expansion.

During the early stages of development, with deficient domestic savings, external financing[16] played a vital role. Two points are worth noting. First, foreign capital should be seen as supplementary, not a substitute, for domestic savings. It can bridge the gap between investment needs and domestic financial capacity, particularly when foreign currency is required to import capital goods essential for industrialization. Second, while external funds can help countries take their first step toward growth, they can also lead to instability if not used wisely. Without building internal savings and productive capacity, countries risk falling into a foreign debt trap.[17]

When domestic financial markets are underdeveloped, entrepreneurs often rely on self-financing as the main source of investment. Business owners use their own savings or borrow privately to build factories and expand production. These entrepreneurs play a crucial role in promoting investment and economic expansion while bearing the full risk of failure. In many cases, family businesses form the foundation of such endeavors. The labor, savings and assets of entire families, and sometimes extended relatives, are pooled together to support new ventures. In the Four Asian Geese, the courage, discipline and determination of these individuals who risked everything to invest were the true driving forces behind economic progress.[18]

However, markets and private firms alone cannot provide large-scale investment for infrastructure, which is essential for industrialization. Governments must take the lead in building power plants, roads, railways, ports, telecommunications, and water systems. These investments increase the economy's productive capacity, raise labor productivity and support technological progress.[19] Without sufficient public investment in infrastructure, rapid and sustained economic growth is almost impossible.

1.3 Limit of the analysis and necessary caution

1.3.1 Fallacy of backward looking

Business bestsellers often promise to distill the secrets of success, but they are weak guides to success in the future. *Jim Collins*'s *Good to Great* and *Tom*

Peters and *Robert Waterman*'s *In Search of Excellence* are classic examples. The former examined 11 firms and the latter 43, with both works identifying common traits that, according to the authors, accounted for the companies' superior performance. Inspired by these books, many managers came to view these traits as formulas to be copied. But ex post evaluations showed that a substantial share of the featured companies failed to outperform thereafter. Between 2001 and 2012, for example, only about half of the *Good to Great cohort* beat the market, and many of the *excellent* firms underperformed. This disappointing record reveals a basic problem. Such books, employing similar modes of analysis, often make the erroneous inference of causation from mere correlation and subsequently treat these correlations as reliable predictors of success.

A similar backward-looking fallacy often appears in cross-country growth analysis. Economists commonly identify a wide range of features shared by successful economies, including advanced infrastructure, high levels of human development, macroeconomic stability, an effective and competent bureaucracy and social inclusion, among others. In practice, some countries that possess many of these attributes nevertheless fail to achieve sustained growth, while others lacking several of them manage to succeed. Studies that focus exclusively on successful countries or firms tend to overlook the numerous cases that adopted similar strategies but did not achieve comparable outcomes. This selection bias can produce a distorted understanding of the factors that truly drive success.

What proves effective in one country or historical period may not yield similar results in another, as historical, political, and cultural conditions vary widely. For example, Japan's postwar industrialization benefited significantly from US assistance and strong global demand during the Cold War. Such circumstances are unlikely to be repeated for developing countries in today's global environment. Backward-looking models therefore risk overgeneralizing from historically specific experiences. Accordingly, attempting to replicate another country's developmental 'playbook' is neither feasible nor reliably effective.

Backward-looking analysis in economics remains valuable for interpreting historical trajectories, but its usefulness for forecasting or policy design is inherently limited. Sustainable economic growth depends less on reproducing the past experiences of others than on adapting fundamental principles, such as productivity enhancement, effective governance, and innovation, to each country's particular conditions and future challenges.

The approach adopted in this book is retrospective, and its conclusions must therefore be understood within this limitation. Readers are cautioned against attempting to replicate the precise pathways followed by the Four Asian Geese. Rather, they are encouraged to examine the underlying drivers of these economies' success. Although empirical studies often offer numerous policy prescriptions for development, many of these are difficult for resource-constrained economies to implement simultaneously. A more practical strategy is to identify a limited number of key drivers which, when carefully adapted to local conditions and implemented in an appropriate sequence, can help transform an economy from poverty to prosperity.[20]

1.3.2 Misunderstanding of causation

Takehiko Nakao, former president of the Asian Development Bank, once remarked "Asia was a region defined by poverty. Half a century later, few would describe it that way. Asia is now widely regarded as an engine of global growth". Nakao highlighted eight conditions that supported the development of the region: reliable energy and transport infrastructure; human development through education and health; macroeconomic stability; an open, market-based economy; competent and accountable public administration; social inclusion; a forward-looking national vision; and political stability and security.

In 2020, the ADB's book, *Asia's Journey to Prosperity*, identified 14 common pillars underpinning the region's development over the past 50 years: the interplay of markets, the state and institutions; the dynamics of structural transformation; modernization of agriculture and rural development; technological progress; education, health and demographic change; investment, savings and finance; infrastructure development; trade, foreign direct investment and openness; macroeconomic stability; poverty reduction and income distribution; gender and development; environmental sustainability and climate change; the role of bilateral and multilateral development finance; and strengthened regional cooperation and integration.

The list of policy recommendations is comprehensive and perhaps nearly exhaustive. If low-income governments were able to implement this entire agenda, sustained economic growth would be highly likely to follow. The difficulty, however, is that poorer countries often lack the fiscal and administrative capacity to act on all fronts simultaneously. Scarce resources necessitate prioritization. Policymakers must routinely confront difficult trade-offs, such as whether to allocate marginal funds to building a bridge, a childcare center or a recycling facility. Few would dispute the importance of climate mitigation, environmental protection, equitable distribution and gender equality. The central question, however, concerns sequencing and focus under conditions of severe constraint.

A deeper problem with extensive policy checklists lies in the frequent confusion between correlation and causation. This error can divert countries onto costly and unproductive paths. Consider structural transformation, commonly defined as the shift from agriculture to manufacturing and subsequently to services, which is often observed alongside economic development. Such transformation is more accurately understood as a consequence rather than a cause of growth. Efforts to engineer structural transformation directly, without establishing the underlying foundations of productivity, are unlikely to succeed and may even prove counterproductive.

Urbanization offers another instructive example. It is often assumed that accelerating urbanization can serve as a strategy for achieving rapid economic growth. Although more urbanized economies tend to exhibit higher income levels, forcing rapid urbanization does not in itself generate prosperity. Instead, it may produce serious social challenges when urban areas lack the capacity to provide employment, housing and adequate public services. It is therefore more appropriate to regard urbanization as a consequence of economic growth rather than its cause.

Technology is widely recognized as a central driver of development, and the postwar rise of Asian economies indeed reflects substantial technological progress. Growth accounting and related empirical research decompose economic growth into contributions from capital, labor and total factor productivity (TFP). Such analyses often attribute a large share of growth to TFP. However, recognizing the importance of TFP does not by itself provide clear guidance to policymakers on how to enhance it. TFP cannot be increased simply through the importation of advanced technology. Rather, it reflects the overall efficiency of an economy, arising from the combined effects of innovation in products and processes, improvements in management practices, stronger institutions and sound public policies. While TFP can be measured after growth has occurred, it cannot easily be identified in advance as a direct policy lever. This characteristic makes it difficult to treat increases in TFP as an independent cause of economic development.

Notes

1 Developing Asia comprises the 46 developing member economies of the Asian Development Bank (ADB), which are further grouped into Central Asia, East Asia, South Asia, Southeast Asia and the Pacific.

2 In this book, Asian countries are grouped into five subregions; East Asia, South Asia, Southeast Asia, Central Asia and the Pacific. Japan, Australia and New Zealand are treated separately. East Asia comprises China, Korea, Mongolia, Taiwan and Hong Kong. South Asia includes India, Maldives, Pakistan, Bangladesh, Sri Lanka, Afghanistan, Nepal and Bhutan. Southeast Asia consists of Brunei Darussalam, Cambodia, Indonesia, the Lao People's Democratic Republic, Malaysia, Myanmar, the Philippines, Singapore, Thailand and Vietnam. Central Asia includes Armenia, Azerbaijan, Georgia, Kazakhstan, the Kyrgyz Republic, Tajikistan, Turkmenistan and Uzbekistan. The Pacific group comprises the Cook Islands, the Federated States of Micronesia, Fiji, Kiribati, the Marshall Islands, Nauru, Niue, Palau, Papua New Guinea, Samoa, the Solomon Islands, Timor-Leste, Tonga, Tuvalu and Vanuatu.

3 Recently Taiwanese companies such as TSMC, Media Tec and UMC have dominated global nonmemory semiconductor market.

4 In the 1980s and 1990s, US Treasury and IMF/World Bank recommended all developing countries with free market policies. The term "Washington Consensus" was first used in 1989 by John Williamson, a former staff member of the International Monetary Fund (IMF) and the World Bank. According to Williamson, the Washington Consensus comprises ten policy recommendations: (i) fiscal

discipline, (ii) public expenditure reform, (iii) tax reform, (iv) financial liberalization toward market-determined interest rates, (v) competitive exchange rates, (vi) import liberalization, (vii) FDI liberalization, (viii) privatization of state-owned enterprises, (ix) deregulation and (x) the protection of property rights. The recommendation were the most frequent answers from economists around Washington DC on what policies would contribute most to growth in Latin America.

5 For example, the US in the 19th century maintained high tariffs to protect its manufacturers, while Germany pursued government-led industrial strategies.

6 Arvind Panagariya, *Free Trade and Prosperity*, Oxford University Press, 2019, p26.

7 However, human capital is a multidimensional concept including health and education. Here, I focus on the quantity and quality of education and skills training. Health and other aspects of human capital are beyond the scope of this report.

8 In empirical studies, education has been defined as number of years spent in schools.

9 Easterly pointed out that even if poor countries substantially expanded their education investments over 1960–2000 and literacy improved, the median growth rate of these countries steadily declined due to corruption, military instability and other factors, Baumol (2007, p126).

10 Condorcet (1743–1794), French Enlightenment movement philosopher and mathematician, put a great emphasis on public education in wider perspective. He asserted that the broader education on social and political principles made the entire society more peaceful, sound and progressive.

11 Asia has been known to have better educated human resources than other regions. However, the data are against the recognition. Until the 1970s, developing Asia's public spending on education was among the lowest in the world: 2.1% of GDP. Over the next four decades, Asia nearly doubled public spending on education. Still in the 2010s, Asia's ratio to GDP was 3.6%, which is far below the average of the world, 4.6%.

12 David E. Bloom, David Canning, Jaypee Sevilla, The Demographic Dividend, Land, 2003, p1.

13 Some Researches suggested that the demographic dividend accounted for between one-fourth and two-fifths of the growth.

14 In the 1960s, Asia's domestic savings rate was 18.0% which was lower than investment rate, 20.4%. Throughout the 1960s, 1970s and 1980s, savings fell short of investments in Asia.

15 Although there is no general agreement on the definition of agricultural land reform, in general, property or cultivating right on farmland is transferred either through compulsory measures or through market transaction with some promotional measures.

16 Foreign direct investment, bank loans, bond purchases and portfolio equity investments by nonresidents were important sources of external finance. The problem of developing countries at the take-off stage are lack of capacity to attract financing resources through these channels. They were less creditworthy to borrow from abroad. Therefore, ODA played major roles.

17 For Brazil, rapid growth in the 1960s and 1970s was financed heavily by external borrowing but collapsed in the early 1980s when debt levels became unsustainable.

18 Yet, entrepreneurs did not act in isolation. They operated within economic and institutional systems that could either support or restrict their efforts. To fully understand the story of economic success, we must look at both the people who took the risks and the systems that enabled their success.

19 Barro, however, found that public domestic investment as a share of GDP has a negative impact on growth. His finding pointed out that large public investment

programs have a negative impact on growth because so many countries manage such investments in ways that are corrupt and inefficient.

20 If the purpose of the analysis is for prediction in the future, authors should define common factors first and divide companies into two groups: one group of companies with and the other without common factors. Then they must analyze mid-term success of two groups, demonstrating that those who have common factors outperform.

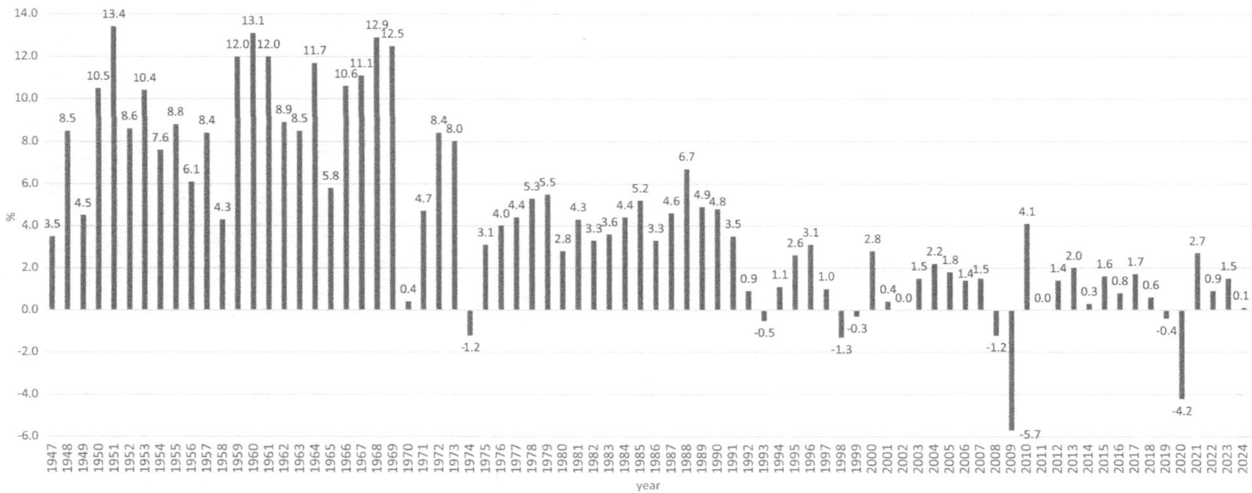

Figure 1 Japan's GDP growth rate (1947–2024).

Sources: GDP growth rates for 1961–2024 are drawn from the World Bank's *World Development Indicators*. Data for the period prior to 1961 are compiled from various domestic statistical sources.

2 Japan, 'Rise of Mt. Fuji'

Japan industrialized and modernized well ahead of its Asian peers. After encounters with Western powers in the 1850s, it was forced to end more than two centuries of isolation. The Meiji Restoration of 1868, which shifted authority from the Tokugawa shogunate to the emperor, supplied the decisive impetus for economic transformation. During the Meiji era (1868–1912), Japan built the political and economic institutions of modern capitalism and, by the early 1900s, joined the ranks of the industrial powers of the world.

Japan's economy was devastated by the Pacific War and defeat, but the postwar reconstruction produced a period of rapid and sustained expansion often described as the 'economic miracle'. From 1950 to 1973, real GDP per capita grew by more than 8% per year. By 1973, per capita income had reached about $22,138, surpassing the United Kingdom and approaching roughly 90% of the United States. Japan reemerged as a leading industrial power, taking global leadership in manufacturing and dominating exports in consumer electronics, automobiles, shipbuilding, machine tools and equipment and, later, semiconductors.

How can Japan's postwar 'economic miracle' be explained? Multiple forces operated in sequence. In the immediate aftermath of the war, US's financial assistance supplied scarce capital, and the Korean War generated external demand that jump-started Japanese industry in the early 1950s. A wide array of structural reforms, including land redistribution, labor market restructuring, the dissolution of large conglomerates, an expansion of educational access, reduced inequality, distributed the gains of growth widely, stabilized society and sustained robust household consumption from the 1950s through the 1970s.

The Japanese government played a central role, particularly in the early postwar years, by actively promoting investment, manufacturing exports and technological upgrading. Beginning in 1955, the government introduced medium-term economic plans that set quantitative targets for overall growth and for sectoral, social, and economic indicators. At the micro level, it implemented targeted industrial policies. The *1960 Income Doubling Plan*, which sought to double per capita income in ten years, achieved its goal in seven

DOI: 10.4324/9781003797135-2

years. Through the 1950s and 1960s, policy priorities deliberately moved from light industries to heavy and chemical industries. The economy turned to high-technology products such as semiconductors, computers, biotechnology and robotics, systematically upgrading manufacturing capabilities and moving up the value chain.

After 1973, Japan's growth rate decelerated for several reasons, including the 1973–1974 and 1979 oil shocks and the forces of convergence as the country reestablished itself as a major industrial economy. Even so, Japan continued to expand significantly faster than most other advanced nations throughout the 1970s and 1980s. From the 1990s onward, however, the bursting of the asset price bubble and rapid aging population produced a further slowdown. Since the late 1990s, confronted with chronic deflation and sluggish growth, Japan has undertaken ambitious structural reforms, including service-sector deregulation, to spur economic growth and address demographic pressures. Nonetheless, the economy has largely stagnated, punctuated only by intermittent episodes of moderate recovery. Multiple fiscal stimulus packages have sought to revive demand, with limited and short-lived effects.

Japan's postwar economic miracle offered a compelling model which provided both practical guidance and psychological confidence for other Asian economies. However, the protracted stagnation after the asset bubble burst in the early 1990s is raising deeper questions about the long-run prospects for growth across the region. Many analysts recommend that Japan should escape stagnation by adopting a focused portfolio of reforms that turns demographic headwinds into productivity gains, reignites private investment and innovation, raises service-sector efficiency, advances green growth and energy security, strengthens the startup and risk-capital ecosystem and modernizes human capital.

2.1 Free and open market economy

2.1.1 Japan, kingdom of bureaucrats?

Some observers describe Japan as a country where the government and its bureaucrats have long dominated politics, the economy and business. This view is especially common among non-Asian commentators. However, those familiar with Japan's history argue that the nation has a deep-rooted tradition of private enterprise and economic initiative.

During *the Shogunate period* (1185–1868),[1] merchants developed advanced and nationwide supply and distribution networks. Large-scale infrastructure projects such as irrigation systems and river transport, both vital for Japan's rice-based economy, were financed and managed by private entrepreneurs. Even before industrialization, the private sector was already at the heart of Japan's economy.

The importance of private enterprise continued under the Meiji Restoration of 1868 which marked the beginning of Japan's industrialization. After more than two centuries of isolation, Japan opened its doors to Western powers in the 1850s and embarked on a national effort to modernize. The government initially established state-owned enterprises (SOEs) in key industries such as textiles, coal and steel, introducing new technologies from the West. Once these industries became viable, however, they were swiftly privatized, signaling a clear intention to let the private sector lead.

For example, electricity in Japan has traditionally been provided by regional private companies, except during the wartime years in 1939–1951. Many of Japan's railway lines were originally built by private merchants, even before the Meiji era, to transport silk and other goods from inland areas to coastal ports. These lines were later nationalized under the Railway Nationalization Act of 1906. Likewise, from the 1910s to the 1930s, private companies built extensive suburban electric railway networks, often alongside new residential, commercial and leisure developments.

The wartime period, especially the Pacific War, significantly expanded the role of bureaucrats in Japan's economy. In preparation for and during the wars, the government intervened in nearly every aspect of economic activity. Strong state control continued after the war to guide reconstruction and address resource shortages. The government implemented targeted industrial policies, focusing on rebuilding key industries and promoting exports. This proactive role gave rise to the widespread, but surely misleading, impression that Japan's economy was dominated by bureaucrats.

The Japanese government generally confined itself to setting broad visions and priorities for industrialization. It avoided direct involvement in production or ownership of businesses. In fact, the government's role was often more about coordination and facilitation than command. It set broad economic goals, maintained macroeconomic stability and created a favorable environment for business to thrive, but the execution and innovation came from the private sector. While the government provided direction and support, it did not always pick winners directly. Instead, it was the market and competition that selected winners. Many industries succeeded through private initiative and competition rather than direct state control. The private sector remained the main engine of economic growth, while the government acted as a facilitator, encouraging investment, supporting exports and fostering technological innovation, especially in the early postwar years.

Japan has long maintained a small government compared to Western nations. Government expenditure has averaged around 30% of GDP, significantly below the roughly 40% typical of Western economies. Japan refrained from large-scale ownership of industrial enterprises or major financial institutions. Most SOEs were concentrated in infrastructure sectors. Over time, Japan pursued continuous privatization, reducing state ownership and improving efficiency. Major examples include the privatization of Nippon Telegraph and Telephone (1985), Japanese National Railways (1987) and Japan Post (2007).

Even in finance, private ownership was dominant. State-owned financial institutions were established only when market gaps existed, often to support specific sectors or small businesses. Most banks, insurance companies and securities firms were privately owned, either as joint-stock corporations or cooperatives serving farmers and small traders. Even public financial institutions enjoyed considerable managerial autonomy, making lending decisions based on commercial criteria rather than political directives.

Importantly, Japan's strong government role did not mean that bureaucrats replaced decisions of private firms or forced them into unwanted ventures. Instead, close cooperation and consultation characterized the relationship between government and business. Bureaucrats frequently exchanged ideas and information with industrial leaders, creating a coordinated system that balanced public goals with private initiative. This collaborative governance model, built on trust and mutual respect, allowed Japan to overcome market imperfections and achieve rapid and sustained economic growth.

2.1.2 Forced opening but a disguised blessing

In July 1853, four American warships under the command of *Commodore Matthew Perry* arrived in Edo Bay and demanded that Japan open its ports to foreign trade. *The Tokugawa Shogunate*, which had enforced a strict policy of national isolation since the early 1600s, refused Perry's request. However, Perry returned the following year with a larger fleet, and under mounting pressure, the Shogun reluctantly agreed to open several ports. Japan's two centuries of isolation effectively came to an end in 1858.

The forced opening of the country divided Japanese society. Many members of the educated middle class opposed the Shogunate's decision and launched a movement for political reform. Their efforts culminated in the Meiji Restoration of 1868, when Shogun *Tokugawa Yoshinobu* resigned and Emperor Meiji ascended the throne. This marked the beginning of Japan's modernization and industrialization.

The new Meiji government introduced sweeping reforms to build modern institutions in education, industry and governance. It also opened the nation to foreign ideas, technologies and systems, actively learning from Western powers. Ironically, many of those who had once resisted Japan's forced opening became the very leaders who guided the country toward modernization and international engagement.

The devastation of World War II left Japan's economy in ruins. The postwar international economic order, however, offered a new and favorable foundation for recovery. Under the systems established by the International Monetary Fund (IMF) and the General Agreement on Tariffs and Trade (GATT),[2] the world economy embraced freer trade and capital movement. Japan joined the GATT in 1955 and became a full member in 1963. During 1955–1970, global trade tripled, growing at an average of 7.6% per year, and

Japan emerged as one of the main beneficiaries of this open and stable international system.

Within the IMF framework, Japan adopted a fixed exchange rate of ¥360 to $1, which supported export expansion and economic growth. Japan joined the IMF in 1952 and became an Article VIII member[3] in 1964, formalizing its commitment to current account convertibility. The undervalued yen boosted exports and attracted foreign capital until 1971, when the fixed exchange rate system was replaced by a floating one. Even afterward, Japan continued to benefit from a relatively weak yen until the Plaza Accord of 1985 brought an end to this advantage.

During the 1960s, Japan deepened its integration into the global economy. The government gradually dismantled trade barriers, import quotas, and restrictions on foreign direct investment. This opening did more than expand trade. It triggered a dramatic rise in productivity. Confronted with intense international competition, Japanese companies worked tirelessly to adopt and improve foreign technologies, eventually developing their own world-class innovations. In the long run, the opening of Japan, initially forced by Western military power, became the foundation for its rise as an industrial and technological leader.

2.2 Accountable government and effective policies

2.2.1 Strategic industrialization by strong coordination

Japan's process of postwar economic growth is often described as the *Asian model*, characterized by a proactive and coordinated role of the government in guiding growth. In the years following World War II, the Japanese government undertook a wide range of structural reforms in major areas, covering land, labor, corporations, education and pensions. These broad reforms laid the groundwork for industrial expansion. Large-scale public investment in infrastructure such as roads, ports and power plants further supported high growth and industrial productivity.[4]

During the 1950s and 1960s, the key economic task of the Japanese government was to ensure sufficient financing for private firms to expand production and exports. It adopted an array of targeted industrial policies that protected and nurtured strategic industries. High tariffs, import quotas and capital controls shielded developing sectors from external competition, while tax incentives such as accelerated depreciation encouraged investment. Domestic banks mobilized savings and directed them to priority industries. Scarce foreign exchange was allocated selectively to firms contributing to export expansion and industrial development.

This system depended on close coordination among three powerful institutions: the Ministry of Finance (MOF), the Bank of Japan (BOJ), and the Ministry of International Trade and Industry (MITI). Together, they implemented industrial policies by managing the supply of domestic credit, access to foreign exchange and incentives for investment. Firms in target industries benefited from low-interest loans, tax advantages, duty-free imports of equipment and protection from foreign competition.[5]

The MOF played a key role in reshaping Japan's financial system after the war. Before the war, large conglomerates (*zaibatsu*) owned major banks and used them to finance their own affiliated companies, often distorting fair competition. Postwar reforms banned such ownership, dispersing bank shares among many smaller investors. The MOF then guided banks to direct loans toward industries critical for national development. In 1957–1974, about 65% of Japan's total industrial capital came from bank loans, far higher than in the United States (6%), the United Kingdom (4%), or Germany (19%).[6] This strong dependence on bank lending reflected the MOF's central role in channeling savings into productive investment and ensuring that financial resources were aligned with the country's broader economic goals.

The BOJ played the role of the monetary enabler, ensuring that credit and liquidity were sufficient to support industrial expansion. Working closely with the MOF, the BOJ used monetary tools to maintain low interest rates and expand the money supply where necessary. One of its most effective policies was the rediscounting of commercial banks' loans that met specific government priorities, such as export promotion or industrial investment. This rediscounting system allowed banks to borrow additional funds from the BOJ, using qualified loans as collateral, which effectively expanded the available credit in the economy.

The MITI, established in 1949, became the core driver of Japan's industrialization. It identified potential 'winner' industries such as steel, shipbuilding, chemicals and machinery and concentrated support on them. These industries were chosen not only for their own growth potential but also for their role in upgrading Japan's industrial structure. Later, MITI expanded its focus to high-technology sectors, including electronics and computers. The ministry also facilitated the importation and diffusion of advanced foreign technologies, improving the competitiveness of Japanese exports. During periods of economic downturn or overcapacity, MITI also intervened to coordinate production cuts and stabilize markets.

All three agencies—the MOF, BOJ and MITI—shared a unified vision of industrialization. Their collaboration exemplified Japan's coordinated capitalism, in which public and private actors worked toward national economic goals. In 1972, then MITI Vice Minister Saburō Ōjimi articulated this strategy by saying "Japan deliberately promoted capital- and technology-intensive industries such as steel, automobiles, petrochemicals, and electronics that appeared unsuitable for Japan's limited resource base. The logic was long-term. These industries offered rapid technological progress, high income elasticity of demand, and fast-rising labor productivity".

2.2.2 *Mobilizing and channeling money*

The Japanese government established several specialized financial institutions to channel both public and private funds into firms operating in high priority sectors. These sectors included export-oriented firms, small- and medium-sized enterprises and industries engaged in modernization and restructuring. Since Japan's capital markets and financial systems were still underdeveloped in the early postwar years, these specialized financial institutions played a crucial role in allocating scarce financial resources. Preferential credit was largely provided through public institutions such as the Development Bank of Japan, the Export–Import Bank of Japan and the Industrial Bank of Japan (IBJ).

The key provider of funds was the Trust Fund Bureau (TFB) at the MOF.[7] TFB was a key financial agency that played an essential role in managing and allocating public savings during Japan's period of rapid economic growth. The primary function of TFB was to collect, manage and invest money deposited in various government-related savings programs. The large part of the fund was mobilized through postal savings, postal life insurance and public pension systems. Instead of being used for ordinary government expenditures, the mobilized funds were pooled within TFB and were allocated to government financial institutions and public corporations.

TFB worked as the financial backbone of the Fiscal Investment and Loan Program (FILP), often called Japan's 'second budget'. While the general government budget covered administrative and operational expenses, FILP financed long-term projects that supported the country's broader economic development. In the early 1950s, FILP was the key mechanism directed public funds toward industrial development. The scale of FILP amounted to roughly 4% of gross national product (GNP) in the 1950s, between 6.5% and 7.5% in the 1970s and 1980s, and exceeded 8% in the early 1990s.

Although its overall size appeared small relative to the total economy, its impact was significant. In 1961, FILP financed 31% of new industrial equipment investments across all sectors. In key industries such as electric power, ocean shipping and coal, it financed about 60% of equipment loans. For the iron and steel industry, FILP accounted for about one-third of total equipment loans in the same year.

In the 1950s, TFB played a particularly important role in supplying long-term financing by purchasing large volumes of debentures issued by long-term credit banks. Operating under MOF, TFB provided funds to policy-based financial institutions such as the Development Bank of Japan, the Export–Import Bank of Japan and the Housing Loan Corporation. Through these institutions, low-cost long-term loans were directed toward priority sectors such as manufacturing, trade and housing.

Among Japan's government-affiliated financial institutions, the Development Bank of Japan and the Export–Import Bank of Japan played particularly influential roles in channeling funds from FILP and TFB to industrial enterprises. In addition, the Small Business Finance Corporation provided financing to small- and medium-sized enterprises, while the People's Finance Corporation extended credit to micro enterprises and newly established firms that faced difficulty in accessing conventional bank lending. Together, these institutions constituted the core of Japan's policy-based financial system.

The IBJ was the largest and most important source of long-term industrial finance during the two decades following the war. Since commercial banks lacked the capacity to provide long-term loans, IBJ filled this critical gap during the reconstruction and high-growth periods. IBJ raised funds by issuing two main types of debentures: one-year discount debentures, mainly purchased by individuals, and five-year coupon debentures, bought primarily by financial institutions. After providing initial loans, the responsibility for monitoring borrowers' performance and repayment was typically delegated to commercial banks.[8]

Importantly, government financial institutions were strictly prohibited from competing directly with private banks and other financial intermediaries. Their role was clearly defined to provide financing to projectors and borrowers who could not access funds on favorable terms through the private financial market. This system ensured that public financial institutions complemented, rather than replaced, private finance, creating a coordinated structure that supported Japan's rapid industrialization and economic growth.

Over time, the total volume and relative importance of policy-based finance continued to grow. Policy finance accounted for about 13% of total lending in the mid-1950s, declined slightly to 10% in the 1960s and then rose again to 15% during the 1970s and 1980s. Despite its modest share, policy-based financing played a pivotal role in supporting industrial investment during Japan's early industrialization period.

2.3 Education and human resource development

2.3.1 Terakoya led to modern education system

Development Economist *Yoshihisa Godo* and *Yujiro Hayami* stressed that Japan's postwar economic success was built on a long history of investment in education. They noted that Japan's accumulated human capital allowed the country to absorb and adapt advanced foreign technologies after the Pacific War, combining these with rapid physical capital investment to achieve high growth.

Indeed, education laid the foundation for Japan's economic miracle. Compulsory primary education was officially introduced in 1886 after the *Meiji Restoration*, but Japan's tradition of schooling went back much further. Long before the modern school system, children attended *Terakoya* which was informal, privately run temple schools that provided basic reading, writing and arithmetic education to commoners.

Terakoya originated in the early 17th century and spread throughout towns and villages, teaching practical literacy and numeracy outside the elite samurai academies. Before their emergence, only the children of samurai and aristocrats had access to formal education, while commoners were largely excluded. *Terakoya* was established by temples, samurai and ordinary citizens who valued learning. By the early 19th century, about 70% of children aged 6–13 attended these schools. At the end of the Edo period, literacy rates were estimated at 50% for men and 20% for women, remarkably high for that time. By the late Edo period, tens of thousands of *Terakoya* existed across Japan. These community-based schools laid the groundwork for Japan's mass literacy and eased the transition to the modern education system after 1872.

In 1872, the Meiji government abolished *Terakoya* through the Education System Order. It replaced them with a national, compulsory elementary school system designed to train skilled manpower for a modern industrial state. The 1886 Primary School Order required all districts to maintain public primary schools, and by 1908 compulsory education was extended from four to six years. By 1910, about 98% of school-age children were enrolled in primary education. These large-scale investments in education before the war created a strong base of human capital that fueled Japan's postwar economic growth.

After World War II, Japan's education system was further reformed. Compulsory education was extended from six to nine years, adding three years of junior high school. In 1950–1970, the average schooling years of the working-age population rose from 7.6 to 9.8 years. From 1890 to 1990, the average schooling in Japan increased by 2.2% per year, three times faster than the 0.7% growth in the United States. In 1955, only 38% of working-age people completed middle school, but by 1965, 58% finished high school and by 1975, the rate reached 91%.

Vocational education was also a major pillar of Japan's industrialization. The Meiji leaders believed that skilled labor was essential to attract foreign technology and investment. Before the Pacific War, the average years of vocational education grew three times faster than general education. The share of vocational students rose from 3% in 1890 to 54% in 1945. This expansion produced the engineers, technicians, managers and clerks required for industrial growth. The vocational training system was institutionally coordinated through collaboration between the ministries responsible for education and labor policy.

To further enhance workforce competencies, the government introduced the National Trade Skill Test in 1959, establishing a standardized system of certification across vocational and technical occupations. In the 1960s, colleges of technology (*Kosen*) were established to provide five-year programs for students aged 15 and older, offering an alternative pathway to conventional high school education. Graduates of *Kosen* were highly sought after by industries such as manufacturing and shipbuilding during the high-growth era. In the 1970s, as industrial needs became more specialized,

Japan expanded its postsecondary vocational education by creating *Senmon Gakko* (specialized training colleges) in 1976. These institutions offered two- to four-year programs focused on practical job skills and complemented the tradition of company-based training.

2.3.2 Lifelong employment and craftsmanship

Japanese society often expresses a strong sense of pride in attaining 'World No. 1' status in areas of excellence, whether in sushi, traditional crafts, toys, paper art or flower arranging. This cultural mindset of striving for excellence dates back centuries. *Oda Nobunaga*, who unified Japan for the first time in the 16th century, once declared, "While we should respect those who are World No. 1, the decision on who deserves that title must reflect the wisdom of all learned men in Kyoto". During this era, craftsmen worked tirelessly to earn the title of being the best in their trade. The honor of being 'No. 1' brought prestige, wealth and lifelong respect. This spirit drove artisans to produce the finest bells, tea utensils, tatami mats and countless other crafts, creating a culture deeply rooted in perfectionism and craftsmanship.

Japan's long tradition of craftsmanship has also produced a remarkable number of enduring companies. Of the approximately 5,586 firms in the world that are more than 200 years old, about 3,146 are in Japan. Japan has over 33,000 firms that are more than a century old. Most of them are small and family-run businesses. Among them, 524 are listed on the Japanese stock market. The world's oldest continuously operating firm, *Kongō Gumi*, a temple construction and repair company, was founded in 578. The abundance of such long-lived companies reflects Japan's deep respect for professionalism, tradition and continuous innovation. Generations of owners and employees have strived to perfect their skills and advance technology while maintaining an unwavering commitment to quality.

Technological progress and productivity improvement have been at the heart of Japan's industrial success. Sony, founded in 1946, began with tape recorders and transistor radios before introducing revolutionary products such as Walkman, flat screen televisions, MP3 players and, later, image sensors and gaming consoles. Toyota, founded in 1937, became one of the world's leading automobile manufacturers through relentless improvement in technology and management systems.

Other examples include Toppan (founded in 1900 for printing), Nihon Densan (1973, precision motors), Mabuchi Motor (1954, small motors), Toray (1926, synthetic fibers), Nitto Denko (1918, tapes and films) and JSR (1957, LCD materials). These firms, through constant innovation, have upheld Japan's global reputation for technological excellence.

While Japan's public education system successfully produced a literate and numerate workforce, it was less effective in supplying workers with practical industrial skills. Japanese firms typically hired young generalists with strong potential rather than specialized skills, then invested heavily in company-specific training. This approach embodied the philosophy of *monozukuri*, which literally means 'making things' but more deeply refers to craftsmanship rooted in field-based learning and continuous improvement. Workers were encouraged to master their craft, refine production techniques and pursue constant efficiency gains.

Japan's greatest strength has been its unique ability to learn from others, adapt foreign technologies and then improve them to fit domestic needs. This process of imitation and innovation was key to Japan's rapid rise. Technological progress in one sector often spreads to others, generating a multiplier effect across industries. For instance, advancements in the steel industry improved the quality of materials used in automobiles, helping Japan's car manufacturers compete globally. Similarly, progress in shipbuilding stimulated growth in related sectors. This inter-industry synergy, driven by a culture of craftsmanship and continuous innovation, became the engine of Japan's extraordinary economic growth.

Japan's system of lifelong employment, which became a hallmark of its postwar economic structure, played a crucial role in building human capital and improving the skill level of its workforce. This employment system was not only a labor practice but also a social contract between companies and employees, based on mutual trust, loyalty and long-term commitment.

Under lifelong employment, workers typically joined a company right after finishing school or university and remained there until retirement. In exchange for job security, employees dedicated themselves fully to the company, often accepting long hours and limited mobility between firms. This stability encouraged companies to invest heavily in training their workers, knowing that such investments would yield long-term returns. Firms provided extensive on-the-job training programs, fostering skills that were highly specific to the company's production methods, technologies and corporate culture. The accumulation of firm-specific skills increased productivity and contributed to the technological innovation that fueled Japan's rapid economic growth in the 1960s to 1980s.[9]

2.4 Savings and investment, leading to capital accumulation

2.4.1 The most successful land reform in the world

General *Douglas MacArthur*, the Supreme Commander of the Allied Powers in Japan, once described Japan's postwar land reform as 'the most successful land reform program in history' in a letter to Prime Minister *Yoshida*. His assessment was not an exaggeration. The reform was both drastic and comprehensive, fundamentally transforming Japan's rural economy and social structure. It transferred land ownership from large landlords to small tenant farmers, dismantling the traditional feudal hierarchy that had dominated Japanese society for centuries. As a result, Japan saw the creation of a large class of independent farmers, which brought greater social equity, reduced rural poverty and strengthened political stability.

Before World War II, agriculture was the backbone of the Japanese economy. In 1880, agriculture and fisheries accounted for around 70% of the labor force and 40% of the nation's net domestic product. Landlordism was widespread. Landlords owned nearly half of all farmlands and held immense economic and social power in rural areas. About 30% of Japan's 5.5 million farming households were pure tenant farmers who worked rented plots, while another 30% owned their land outright, and the remaining 40% were mixed cultivators working both owned and rented fields. Most tenant farmers cultivated less than 0.3 hectares of land and paid nearly half their harvest as rent. For example, in the 1930s, out of every 3.5 tons of rice produced per hectare, 1.7 tons went to the landlord.

Efforts to improve the plight of tenant farmers began even before the war. The *Meiji* government provided financial support to help tenants purchase land and introduced a two-tier pricing system that allowed them to buy land at lower prices. The 1939 law that capped land rents further weakened landlord dominance. These reforms led to gradual improvements in ownership and productivity, setting the stage for future agricultural modernization.

However, during the two World Wars, much of this progress was reversed. By the end of World War II, half of Japan's farmland was cultivated by tenants, and food shortages intensified as a result of wartime destruction and the disruption of rice imports. In response, land reform became an urgent national priority. Two major reforms followed: the first was initiated by the Japanese government in December 1945, and the second, more comprehensive reform was implemented under the US occupation between 1946 and 1950 under the supervision of General MacArthur.[10]

The postwar land reform laws mandated the compulsory purchase of all land owned by absentee landlords and any tenanted land exceeding five hectares.[11] The traditional rent-in-kind system was replaced with much lower cash rents. The government purchased land from landlords at fixed 1945 prices and resold it to tenants on favorable terms, either in cash or in 30-year installments with low interest. Due to hyperinflation in the late 1940s, the real value of payments fell dramatically, making land acquisition affordable for farmers. For instance, one *tan* (0.099 hectares) of paddy land worth the equivalent of 3,000 packs of cigarettes in 1939 cost only about 13 packs in 1948. The results were remarkable. The proportion of 'owner cultivators increased from 31% in 1941 to 70% in 1955, while the share of 'tenant farmers' declined markedly from 28% to 4%. The number of 'mixed tenants' also declined sharply. Absentee landlords virtually disappeared, and tenancy rights were strengthened.

Japan's land reform was a cornerstone of its postwar economic take-off. By giving farmers ownership of their land, it created powerful incentives for productivity and innovation. Farmers invested in fertilizers, tools and better farming techniques, increasing agricultural output and generating surplus savings. These savings, in turn, supported Japan's industrialization by providing capital for private investment and education. Many farmers' children, educated with the help of this new wealth, became part of Japan's skilled industrial workforce. In this way, the land reform achieved far more than a simple redistribution of land. It redistributed opportunity and laid the social and economic foundation for Japan's postwar recovery and rapid growth.

2.4.2 Postal savings, World No.1

Across Japan, post offices serving as deposit centers once far outnumbered all bank head offices and branches combined.[12] It was not until 1990 that the number of bank branches finally surpassed post offices. The origins of this vast network date back to 1871, when the Meiji government introduced the postal savings system, modeled after Great Britain's post office savings scheme. It proved remarkably effective in mobilizing domestic capital, as it utilized the extensive network, which already reached every part of the country. Even households in remote rural areas could easily use financial services through their local post office. Between 1905 and 1914, postal savings increased fourfold. After World War II, postal savings became Japan's main household savings channel and a key source of funding for public investment during the nation's high-growth period.

The postal savings system thrived not only because of its nationwide reach but also because it enjoyed favorable tax[13] and regulatory treatment from the government. It offered depositors more flexibility than private banks, such as allowing multiple accounts under fictitious names and longer-term deposit options. Until 1971, while banks could offer maturities of up to one-year, postal savings provided deposit terms of up to ten years, making it a more attractive option for long-term savers.[14]

During the postwar period, particularly from the 1950s to the 1970s, postal savings played a vital role in financing Japan's rapid economic growth. The funds supported key sectors such as industry, housing, transportation and energy, making the system a cornerstone of Japan's development strategy. By the late 20th century, the postal savings system had become one of the largest financial institutions in the world. However, it faced criticism for inefficiency and excessive government control. To address these issues, Prime Minister Junichiro Koizumi initiated reforms, and Japan Post was privatized beginning in 2007 to make it more transparent and competitive.

In 2007, the postal savings system was reorganized and divided into four entities: Japan Post Holdings, Japan Post Bank, Japan Post Insurance and Japan Post Co., marking the start of gradual privatization.[15] By 2008, Japan Post Bank[16] became the world's largest deposit-holding institution, with assets totaling $1.9 trillion, roughly 25% of Japan's total deposits and nearly three times that of the world's largest private bank.

Japan's high savings rate was also supported by favorable demographics. A growing working-age population, rapid economic growth and government savings policies all contributed to rising savings levels. The gross domestic savings rate increased from about 24% of GDP in 1955 to 42% in 1970, while domestic investment rose from 24% to 41% of GDP during the same period. This strong link between high savings and investment fueled rapid capital accumulation, industrial upgrading and productivity growth.

Although domestic savings provided the foundation for Japan's economic expansion, external financing also played a crucial supplementary role in meeting the country's large capital needs. After World War II, Japan received international aid, mostly from the US, in the form of food, clothing and agricultural supplies. More significantly, the International Bank for Reconstruction and Development (IBRD) provided Japan with large project loans totaling $863 million between 1951 and 1966. These loans financed the development of Japan's 'Pacific Belt Zone', an industrial corridor stretching from Tokyo to Fukuoka. Major projects funded included the Yawata Iron & Steel Company (1955), the Toyota Motor Koromo Plant (1956), the Kansai Electric Power Hydroelectric Station (1958), the Tokaido Shinkansen (1961) and the Tomei Expressway (1964).

Notes

1 The Shogunate period in Japan refers to the time when the country was governed by military rulers known as shoguns instead of the emperor. It lasted from 1185 to 1868 and included three major shogunates: the Kamakura Shogunate (1185–1333), Ashikaga Shogunate (1336–1573) and e Tokugawa Shogunate (1603–1868). Shogunate period ended in 1868 with the Meiji Restoration, when power was returned to the emperor and Japan began its rapid modernization.

2 The GATT was established in 1947 as an international agreement aimed at reducing tariffs and other trade barriers to promote free and fair trade among member countries. It functioned primarily as a set of rules and negotiations rather than a formal organization. Over time, GATT helped lower global trade barriers through several "rounds" of negotiations. The World Trade Organization (WTO) was created in 1995 as part of the Uruguay Round of GATT negotiations. The WTO took over and expanded GATT's functions.

3 Article VIII membership reflects a country's readiness to operate a stable, open and convertible exchange system in line with international norms.

4 For example, paved roads increased from 23,800 to 511,000 kilometers during 1960–1970, and annual electricity generating capacity increased from 23.7 million to 68.3 million kilowatts during 1960–1980.

5 Michael Schumsn, *The Miracle*, 2009, Happer Business, p13.

6 Bai Gao, *Japan's Economic Dilemma*, 2001, Cambridge Press, p86.

7 As Japan's financial system matured, the government introduced reforms in the late 1990s to improve transparency and reduce bureaucratic dominance in public finance. In 2001, the Trust Fund Bureau was dissolved, and its functions were transferred to the newly created Fiscal Loan Fund, designed to manage public funds in a more transparent and market-oriented way.

8 Long-term credit banks also accepted deposits from financial institutions and from their own clients, but they were not permitted to take deposits from the public.

9 However, the system also had limitations. It was most effective in large corporations and manufacturing industries but less so in smaller firms or the service sector. It also discouraged labor mobility, potentially limiting innovation from outside talent. Moreover, as Japan's economy matured and growth slowed in the 1990s, maintaining lifetime employment became increasingly difficult due to rising labor costs and global competition.

10 Although the reform was directed by US occupation forces, Japanese Ministry of Agriculture, even before the war, drafted a comprehensive land reform plan which was used as the basis for the reform program under US occupation. This was critical for the success of the reform.

11 The second land reform on October 11, 1946, decreased to 3 hectares.

12 They included city banks, regional banks, trust banks, long-term credit banks, sogo banks and shinkin banks.

13 Small deposits at all banks were exempt from income tax.

14 Maturity of deposits could be extended to up to three years.

15 Japan Post Bank (JP Bank), a listed retail bank, still distributes through roughly 24,000 post offices and around 30,000 ATMs, serving many elderly and rural customers, and, as of March 31, 2025, it reports roughly ¥233.5 trillion in assets and about ¥190 trillion in deposits while the government continues to reduce its indirect stake over time to bolster independence and competition with private banks.

16 Postal saving system was criticized for its dominance over private banking. The negative outcome of the Postal Office's dominance in savings was underdevelopment of financial system and diverting accumulated funds in less efficient industries instead of new industries. In October 2005, Japan passed the law to execute privatization of postal system. The Japanese postal system was divided into four separate entities; Japanese Post Holdings, Japan Post, Yu-cho Bank and Kan-po Life Insurance.

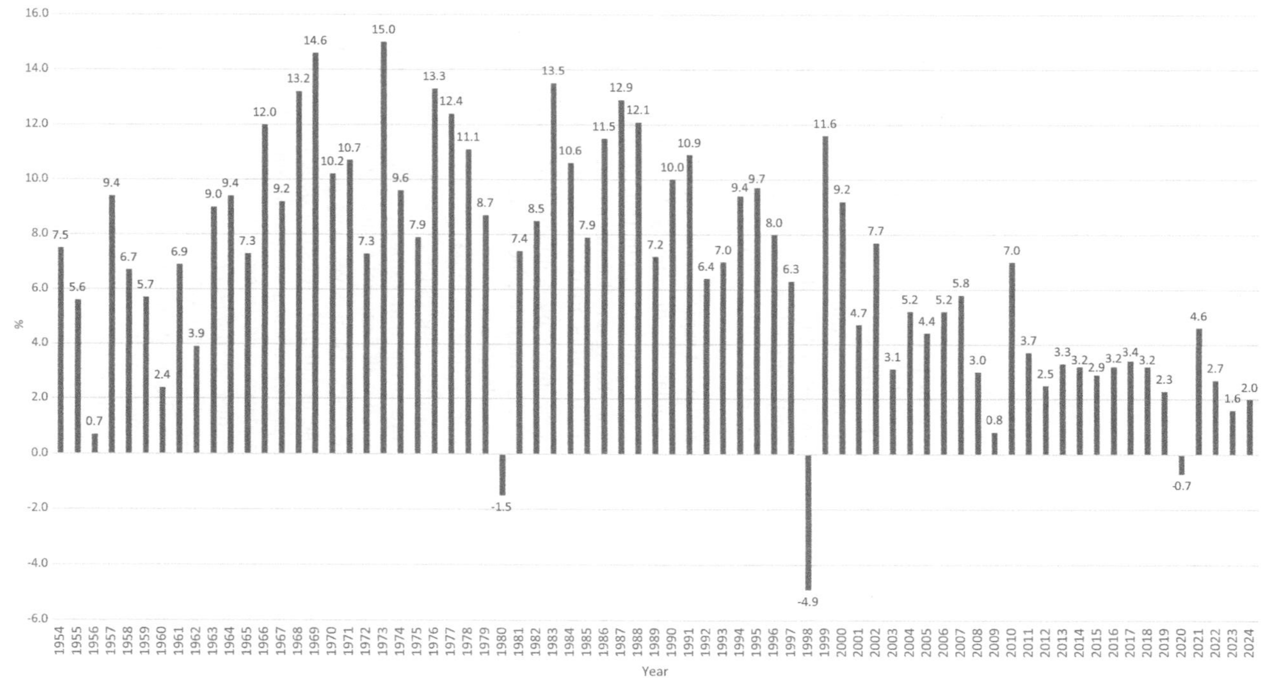

Figure 2 Korea's GDP growth rate (1954–2024).

Sources: GDP growth rates for 1961–2024 are drawn from the World Bank's *World Development Indicators*. Data for the period prior to 1961 are compiled from various domestic statistical sources.

3 Korea, 'Miracle on the Han River'

Eighty years ago, Korea was among the poorest countries in the world. After Japan's surrender in 1945, Korea regained independence and established its first modern government in 1948. Divided between a US-administered South and a Soviet-administered North, the peninsula soon descended into the Korean War (1950–1953), which devastated farmland and reduced industrial assets on both sides to ruins. When the armistice took effect in 1953, South Korea's per capita GDP was just $67 and even by 1961, on the eve of take-off, it had risen only to $82.

From the early 1960s, Korea sustained rapid growth for several decades. Exports expanded at an average annual rate of roughly 40% during 1962–1970, and real GDP grew by an average of 7.5% from 1962 to 2000. By the 1980s, Korea joined Singapore, Hong Kong and Taiwan as one of the 'Asian Tigers'. Per capita GDP surpassed $30,000 in 2019, and by 2020 the country ranked as the world's tenth largest economy by nominal GDP. Korean firms now stand at the forefront of high-tech industries, including semiconductors, electronics, ICT, automobiles and biochemicals.

Multiple factors underpinned this expansion including economic planning backed by strong leadership and a capable bureaucracy, ample and low-cost labor, high domestic savings, bold private investment by entrepreneurial firms, prudent fiscal policy combined with financial repression and relatively equal income distribution. Unlike many Asian developing peers, the Korean government played an activist role in guiding industrial development. That intervention, however, also produced distortions such as an underdeveloped financial sector, overinvestment and excessive leverage and the concentration of economic power in large conglomerates (*chaebol*).

Korea suffered a major setback during the Asian financial crisis of 1997, triggered by imprudent investments financed through heavy foreign currency borrowing. The government responded with corporate and financial restructuring and a shift toward a more open, market-oriented system, allowing the economy to recover comparatively quickly. People often say the 1997 economic and financial crisis was a blessing in disguise. Today, however, Korea faces renewed headwinds. The advantages that once powered growth have

DOI: 10.4324/9781003797135-3

largely eroded. Labor is no longer cheap and abundant. Income distribution has become less equal. The education system produces too few creative, job-ready professionals. Entrepreneurial dynamism has weakened.

These factors have contributed to a marked slowdown in growth. The average annual rate fell from 7.5% in 1962–2000 to 4.7% in 2001–2007, 3.2% in 2008–2011 and about 2.0% in 2011–2023. Looking ahead, the OECD projects that annual growth may fall to around 1%–2% by the 2030s. While this change reflects the country's natural transition from a rapidly industrializing economy to a mature and high-income one, Korea is facing deeper structural challenges related to demographics, productivity and global dependence. Additionally, Korea's heavy dependence on exports makes it vulnerable to external shocks such as trade disputes or global demand fluctuations, while high household debt and rising income inequality have limited domestic consumption and overall economic vitality.

Whether and how the Korean economy can regain the higher growth of the 1960s–1980s remains an open question, closely tied to the longer-term effectiveness and renewal of economic planning and export-driven strategies. Korea is often praised for achieving industrialization and democratization concurrently, joining the ranks of advanced economies and transforming from an aid recipient into a donor. Looking ahead, however, the Korean economy must chart its own creative path to growth, as the Japanese model and other past templates no longer offer a reliable guide.

3.1 Free and open market economy

3.1.1 Diverging paths of South and North Korea

Before Korea was divided at the end of World War II in 1945, there was little difference in the level of economic development between the North and the South. Both regions shared a similar agricultural base, comparable income levels and a largely homogeneous society.[1] However, after the division, the two Koreas embarked on radically different paths of economic development. South Korea adopted an open, market-oriented economic system, while North Korea pursued a closed, centrally planned communist system. Starting from the same point, the outcomes after 80 years are strikingly different. Today, South Korea is over 30 times wealthier than North Korea.

In the years immediately following the division, North Korea was more developed than the South. In the early 1960s, South Korea's per capita GDP was only $92, while North Korea's was $151. The North also possessed most of the peninsula's natural resources, including coal, iron ore and hydroelectric capacity. Eighty-six percent of total power generation was concentrated there, compared to just 14% in the South. Yet by the early 1970s, South Korea overtook North Korea in per capita income, and by 2019, South Korea's per capita GDP rose to over $30,000, while North Korea's stood at roughly $1,000. Life expectancy in South Korea now exceeds that of North Korea by more than ten years, symbolizing a profound economic and social divergence.

The fundamental reason for this divergence lies in the two countries' contrasting economic systems. As economists *Daron Acemoglu* and *James Robinson* argue, South Korea's success is rooted in its inclusive institutions that protect property rights and encourage market participation, while North Korea's failure stems from its extractive, centrally planned regime that suppresses private initiative. With support from the US, South Korea established a market economy recognizing private property and competition. By contrast, North Korea, under Soviet influence, outlawed private ownership and abolished markets, leaving citizens with no incentive to increase productivity or innovate.

Two key moments shaped the introduction of market mechanisms in South Korea after independence. First, properties left behind by the Japanese after World War II were sold to private individuals and companies at market prices under US military administration. During the US military governance in 1945–1948, Korea's national affairs were managed under the principle of privatization. Assets such as farmland, factories and enterprises formerly owned by Japanese settlers were sold to Koreans. The first Korean government after 1948 continued these policies, transferring a large share of industrial assets to private hands.[2] Second, farmland was redistributed from large landlords to small farmers through land reform, not as a free giveaway but with reasonable compensation. These measures expanded private ownership and encouraged a more dynamic private sector, dismantling rigid class structures and promoting upward social mobility. Farmers were motivated to improve productivity, invest in better tools and fertilizers and educate their children, laying the foundation for future human capital accumulation.[3]

In North Korea, the Land Reform Law of March 1946 took a far more radical approach. Landlords, both Japanese and Korean, who owned more than 50,000 square meters of land were expropriated without compensation. The confiscated land was distributed free of charge to poor tenant farmers, and the tenancy system was abolished. Initially, the reform was extremely popular, as most North Koreans were impoverished farmers who suddenly gained ownership of their land. This won widespread support for *Kim Il Sung*'s regime, which consolidated political power through the reform.

However, the system of private landownership in North Korea was short-lived. In 1954–1958, the regime replaced private farms with collective farms under state control. Farmers became employees of collective units, and private property rights were eliminated. Without personal ownership or market incentives, agricultural productivity declined. The collectivization process erased the initial benefits of land reform and led to widespread inefficiency and food shortages.

The contrasting experiences of the two Koreas demonstrate how deeply political and institutional choices shape economic outcomes. South Korea's system of private property, market incentives and openness to trade unleashed individual initiative and productivity, driving one of the most remarkable economic transformations in modern history. North Korea's rigid collectivism and suppression of markets, on the other hand, resulted in chronic stagnation and poverty.

3.1.2 From wigs to semiconductors

Today, Korea's export structure is led by advanced, high-technology products such as semiconductors, mobile phones, automobiles, chemicals and ships, produced by globally recognized firms like Samsung, Hyundai, LG, SK and POSCO. However, in the 1960s, Korea's main export was wigs. With few natural commodities to export, the country turned to wigs as a practical export item because human hair was readily available and self-replenishing. Wig exports were only about $14,000 in 1964 but surged to roughly $93 million by 1970, accounting for nearly 10% of Korea's total exports.

To the surprise of many, export-led growth was not South Korea's original strategy for economic growth. In the 1950s and early 1960s, global economic thinking and policy advice from international organizations favored import-substitution industrialization, which aimed to protect domestic producers by restricting competing imports. Korea followed this approach during the 1950s. Although the government made some effort to promote exports, these were mainly viewed to earn foreign currency for importing essential goods. Because foreign exchange was scarce, Korea maintained strict import controls, high tariffs and an overvalued exchange rate. Exports in the late 1950s averaged only about $20 million per year, while imports were roughly $370 million.[4]

The first Korean government, established in 1948, lacked a clear development strategy. Its priority was to stabilize the economy and prevent famine. The Korean War (1950–1953) caused severe economic disruption, and policies during the 1950s focused on rehabilitation. Imports of food, fertilizer and fuel were financed largely through foreign aid, especially from the US. With little foreign exchange, the government adopted import-substitution policies, banning most imports and maintaining an overvalued currency.

Trade restrictions had been tightened over time. In 1946, import–export licensing was introduced, allowing imports only for specific items and banning the export of essential domestic goods. In 1949, import quotas were added, and in 1955 a 'positive list' system was introduced, meaning that only items explicitly approved could be imported. This gave authorities wide discretion in approving or restricting imports, often based on political or administrative considerations.

When President *Park Chung Hee* came to power in 1961, he launched an ambitious economic plan. Initially, it emphasized import substitution due to chronic shortages of foreign currency. Korea lacked domestic resources such as steel, coal and energy and had insufficient funds to import these essentials. President Park was deeply concerned about the uncertainty of foreign aid. The only way to finance imports was to earn foreign exchange through exports. As a result, Korea shifted from import substitution to an export-oriented strategy. This shift was not optional. Rather, it was a matter of survival.

Export promotion did not imply immediate trade liberalization. Instead, while the government actively encouraged exports through various incentives, imports continued to be strictly controlled. In 1965, exporters were granted greater freedom to import raw materials through generous wastage allowances. This privilege was highly valued, as most imports were otherwise restricted or heavily taxed. The more a company achieved in export performance, the greater its import allowances became. Firms that managed to save imported materials during production could sell the surplus on the domestic market, often earning substantial profits.

Interestingly, as Korea transitioned to export-led growth, its average tariff rate initially increased from about 35% in 1957 to nearly 57% in 1968. This was because, under import substitution, most imports were banned and tariffs had little practical effect. Once imports were allowed to support export production, tariffs became a policy tool for managing the balance of payments.[5]

As exports grew and the balance of payments improved in the mid-1960s, trade gradually opened. Korea joined the General Agreement on Tariffs and Trade (GATT) in 1967 and introduced a 'negative list system' under which imports were generally allowed unless specifically prohibited. The share of liberalized imports expanded through the late 1960s and 1970s. By easing import restrictions step by step, Korea steadily deepened its openness to global trade.

The government offered extensive support to export-oriented industries through long-term credit, tax incentives, vocational training and R&D funding. Two characteristics stood out. First, export financing carried much lower interest rates than ordinary business loans. In 1966–1972, the average commercial loan rate was 23.2%, while export loans were available at the rate of 6.1%. Second, foreign exchange policy was redesigned to support exports. In the 1950s, Korea's currency had been kept overvalued to reduce import costs for the government. The government reversed this by adopting a gradual devaluation policy. In 1960–1961, the official exchange rate was sharply adjusted, and by 1965, the Won, the Korean currency, depreciated to roughly one-fifth of its earlier value. Continued currency devaluation in 1968–1971 made exports more competitive and helped lessen the economy's reliance on imports.

Exports have been the principal driver of Korea's economic growth for the past five decades. This would not have been possible without the transformation of its export structure from simple consumer goods to capital goods and high-technology products. The diversification and expansion of export items stimulated competition and encouraged innovation across emerging industries. As *Adam Smith* observed, "The division of labor is limited by the extent of the market". Korea's experience demonstrates that the larger the market, the greater the opportunities for specialization, efficiency and sustained innovation.

3.2 Accountable government and effective policies

3.2.1 Military coup led to economic take-off

At dawn on May 16, 1961, General *Park Chung Hee* and his allies executed a carefully planned military coup that had been in preparation for over a year. General Park moved to the Sixth District Army Headquarters to direct the operation and addressed his soldiers with a rallying call. "We shall rise up to save the country". By 4:15 a.m., after a brief clash with police guards, Park's forces crossed the Han River and seized key government buildings in central Seoul. Soon after, they proclaimed the establishment of the Military Revolutionary Committee and declared their takeover of power.

Park Chung Hee assumed the presidency in 1963 and remained in office for the subsequent 18 years, serving five consecutive terms until his assassination in October 1979. During this period, South Korea experienced rapid economic growth and began to move beyond widespread poverty, laying the foundations for a modern industrial economy. Although his legacy remains contested because of his authoritarian rule, both domestic and international observers generally acknowledge his decisive role in the country's economic transformation. Under his leadership, a series of economic reforms was introduced, leading to a substantial rise in investment from 9.7% of GDP in 1961–1962 to 15.3% in 1963–1966, and an increase in annual GDP growth from 3.9% to 9.2% over the same periods.

For President Park, economic success was crucial for his political survival by getting people's support in two respects. First, he needed to legitimize his regime, which had begun through a military coup, by delivering tangible economic results. He promised rapid economic recovery to gain public support and consolidate his power. Second, he viewed economic strength as essential for national security, particularly in countering the threat posed by North Korea, which at that time was economically and militarily superior to the South.

President Park justified his coup as a move to replace what he called an 'incompetent and corrupt government'. The first administration, led by President *Rhee Syngman* from 1948 to 1960, struggled with political instability, ideological conflict and the aftermath of the Korean War. Industrialization was beyond its reach, and the government failed to achieve meaningful economic restoration. The second administration, under President *Jang Myun*, took office after the student-led April Revolution ousted Rhee for electoral fraud, but it lasted only one year and had no chance to introduce an economic development strategy.[6]

In fact, economic planning was not a new idea under President Park. The concept had been discussed since the early 1950s. The first formal plan, the Seven-Year Economic Development Plan of 1953, aimed to rebuild the war-torn economy, drawing heavily from the report of United Nations Korean Reconstruction Agency, 'An Economic Program for Korean Reconstruction' (known as *the Nathan Report*). It was an excellent and comprehensive plan, but President Rhee dismissed it due to his distrust of centralized economic planning.

In 1953–1961, Korea's economy grew at an annual rate of about 3.8%. Though not disastrous, this growth fell far short of the country's potential. Many observers noted that this growth stemmed more from rent-seeking activities than from productive investment.[7] Most businesses expanded by acquiring Japanese assets at bargain prices, winning non-competitive public contracts, securing access to cheap policy loans and foreign currencies and exploiting import quotas and licenses. Political and bureaucratic connections were often more important than innovation or efficiency.

Korea's subsequent transformation under Park demonstrated how strong government leadership can play a decisive role in economic development. President Park provided a clear, long-term vision and personally monitored progress. He chaired two regular meetings every month: one on export expansion and another on overall economic performance. Over his 18 years in office, he rarely missed these sessions except when traveling abroad. These meetings allowed business leaders to directly raise obstacles they faced, and Park often resolved issues immediately by ordering relevant ministers to take corrective action.

Park's leadership was supported by a disciplined and technocratic bureaucracy. In 1963, the government established the Economic Planning Board (EPB) to coordinate national development planning and oversee the formulation and implementation of economic policy. The EPB was headed by a minister-level official who, from 1967 onward, concurrently served as Deputy Prime Minister for Economic Affairs. It maintained close coordination with the President's economic advisors and ensured policy coherence across economic ministries. Most senior officials were recruited through highly competitive, merit-based examinations, thereby reinforcing professionalism and continuity in economic management.

3.2.3 Five-Year Economic Development Plans

Most economists and policymakers regard year 1962 as the true beginning of Korea's economic miracle. Why? Because it was the year when 'the First Five-Year Economic Development Plan' was launched. Throughout the 1960s and 1970s, the Five-Year Plans served as both a blueprint and a roadmap for Korea's industrialization and solid infrastructure, leading to economic growth. They became the central instrument through which the government played its leading role in transforming a war-torn agricultural economy into an industrial powerhouse. The Five-Year Plans provided long-term direction for both policymakers and business leaders. They mobilized scarce resources and channeled them into strategic sectors. By combining government planning with private sector dynamism, Korea was able to sustain rapid industrialization.

The First Five-Year Plan (1962–1966) focused on developing industries serving basic needs of consumers, farmers and other industries such as cement, fertilizer, machinery and oil refining. Initially centered on import substitution, the plan soon pivoted toward export promotion when policymakers realized that a shortage of foreign currency was the main obstacle to industrial expansion. These measures helped exports soar from $55 million in 1962 to $478 million by 1970, while GDP growth averaged nearly 9% annually.

The Second Five-Year Plan (1967–1971) started to emphasize heavy and chemical industries, including steel, machinery, petrochemicals and shipbuilding. Policymakers understood that Korea needed a new engine for growth beyond labor-intensive light industries. The government encouraged firms to invest in these capital-intensive sectors by offering low-interest loans and tax benefits. The construction of Pohang Iron and Steel Company (POSCO) in 1968 symbolized Korea's ambition to move into more advanced, capital-intensive industries.

In the 1970s, the Third (1972–1976) and the Fourth (1977–1981) Five-Year Plans marked the high point of state-led industrialization through the Heavy and Chemical Industry (HCI) drive. The government aimed to move up the technological ladder and strengthen national security by developing core industries such as steel, shipbuilding, machinery, automobiles and petrochemicals. Massive investments were directed into these strategic sectors through state-controlled banks and policy loans at low interest rates.

During the 1980s, the Fifth (1982–1986) and the Sixth (1987–1991) Five-Year Plans shifted focus from expansion to stabilization and technological upgrading. After the heavy industrial drive of the 1970s led to overcapacity and heavy debt, the government emphasized macroeconomic stability, financial liberalization and efficiency. Korea began to prioritize technology-intensive sectors such as electronics, semiconductors and precision machinery, fostering innovation and productivity. The private sector, supported by government policy, increasingly led growth through investment in research and development.

Why, then, did the Five-Year Plans under President Park succeed when earlier attempts in 1950s failed? The answer lies in political stability, strong leadership and disciplined execution. President Park's government held policy consistency and relied on capable technocrats to ensure thorough implementation. Disciplined and capable bureaucrats in the EPB and related ministries turned national goals into detailed, actionable programs under the strong leadership. The most striking element for success was the support of the Korea Development Institute (KDI) by conducting economic analysis and evaluating policies more systematically. KDI, established in 1971 as a government-affiliated think tank, provided expertise in economic policy research, planning and long-term forecasting. KDI quickly became the central institution responsible for drafting, assessing and refining subsequent Five-Year Economic Development Plans, beginning with the Third Plan (1972–1976).

The most successful, at the same time controversial, example of Five-Years Plans was the launch of the HCI drive in the 1970s and 1980s. The shift was driven by two main reasons. First, Korea needed to climb the technological ladder and move beyond dependence on low-value light manufacturing. Second, facing growing uncertainty about continued US military protection, the country aimed to build a stronger national defense through the development of heavy industries. The idea started in the Second Plan and comprehensive planning and consistent execution of this strategy were carried out through the following Five-Year Plans for the next decade. So, the Five-year Plans enabled Korea to transform its economy with longer-term vision.

3.3 Education and human resource development

3.3.1 Tower of cow bones

In Korea during the 1960s and 1970s, a college diploma was often referred to as a *tower of cow bones*. This expression reflected the deep sacrifices which families made for their children's education. At that time, Korea was still an agricultural society, and cows were among the most valuable assets for farmers, essential for plowing fields and breeding calves. Nevertheless, parents were willing to sell even their most precious cows to pay for their children's college tuition. A typical four-year college education required the equivalent value of four cows, symbolizing immense parental devotion and the nation's intense commitment to education.

Education has always held the highest priority in Korean society. Throughout its 2,000-year history, Korea has maintained a deep respect for scholars and teachers, who are regarded with the same reverence as King and Father. This tradition was rooted in Confucian philosophy, which placed learning at the center of personal and social advancement. Education has always functioned as a key pathway for upward mobility, allowing individuals and families to rise above social and economic barriers that had persisted for centuries. Teachers were among the most respected professionals, and the brightest high school graduates often chose to attend teachers' colleges.

It is widely acknowledged that Korea's rapid economic development over the past six decades was strongly supported by massive investment in human capital. Educational expansion provided a steady supply of highly skilled labor, which fueled productivity growth in manufacturing and other sectors. Beyond economic gains, education also strengthened nation-building and social cohesion by nurturing informed and responsible citizens. Furthermore, education served as the most effective means of promoting equality and social mobility. Families moved across the country in search of better schools, creating both social and regional mobility. During the high-growth era of the 1960s to 1980s, Korea maintained one of the lowest levels of income inequality in the world.[8]

The question arises. How was this massive supply of educated and skilled human capital made possible? Three main factors contributed: demographic change, household spending on education and government investment in public schooling.

First, demographic change played an important role. Like many developing countries during their take-off stages, Korea had a large young population, which could be an asset if properly educated and employed. However, without sufficient education, rapid population growth could easily turn into a burden, consuming resources and hindering savings. Korea's fertility rate remained above 4% until 1960, and the population grew rapidly at nearly 6% per year, even amid postwar hardship. This growth was further fueled by migration from Japan, China and North Korea. The baby boom generation,[9] born between 1955 and 1962, provided abundant labor for the country's new industries. Fearing that overpopulation could hamper economic growth, the government launched an aggressive family planning campaign, offering free birth control and sterilization services and legalizing abortion in 1973.

Second, Korean households consistently prioritized education over all other expenditures. Education was viewed as the surest way to secure a better future, and parents were determined to send their children to the best schools possible. Families relocated to neighborhoods known for high-quality schools, driving up housing prices and overcrowding in those areas. In the 1960s, competition centered on middle school entrance exams; in the 1970s, on high school admissions; and from the 1980s onward, on university entrance exams. Private tutoring became widespread, and spending on private education often accounted for around 30% of total household expenses.

Third, the Korean government made heavy investments in public education. Just one year after the Korean War ended, the government launched the Six-Year Plan for compulsory primary schooling (1954–1959) and the results were dramatic. Despite the financial burden of postwar reconstruction and industrialization, the government continued to allocate significant resources to building schools and expanding access to education. The illiteracy rate dropped from 78.2% in 1948 to just 4.1% in 1958. Educational investment grew steadily afterward. Primary education became free and compulsory in 1954, and middle school education followed in 2003. The primary school enrollment rate rose from 88.9% in 1965 to 100% by the 1990s. Middle school enrollment increased from 30.6% in 1965 to 96.2% in 2009, while tertiary enrollment jumped from 4.4% in 1965 to an impressive 70.4% in 2009, the highest among OECD countries.

As Korea's economy advanced, educational investment expanded to higher education. A comparison with the Philippines illustrates this point. By

2005, both countries had achieved near-universal primary education, with enrollment rates around 100%. However, Korea far outpaced the Philippines in secondary and tertiary education. From 1970 to 2005, Korea's secondary enrollment rate rose from 38.0% to 93.0%, while the Philippines' rose from 32.3% to 83.3%. In tertiary education, Korea's enrollment increased from 8.0% to 71.3%, compared to 19.9% to 28.0% in the Philippines. While economic development certainly played a role in expanding higher education, Korea's steadfast investments in education at all levels was itself a fundamental driving force behind the nation's rapid economic growth.

3.3.2 Seven consecutive wins of World Skills Competition

For Koreans, there are three major Olympic events. The first two are the well-known Summer and Winter Olympic Games, while the third is the *Skills Olympics*, officially known as *the World Skills Competition*. One of Korea's greatest sources of national pride is that it won this competition eight consecutive times between 1971 and 1984. Many Koreans viewed success in the World Skills Competition as a reflection of the country's rapid industrialization and technological advancement.

In Korea, education was not regarded merely as a means of academic achievement but as a practical ladder to better employment. The government continuously sought to align the education system with the evolving needs of the economy. During the early 1960s, when Korea's economy was still at the stage of labor-intensive industrialization, primary education provided essential skills such as literacy, numeracy and discipline. In the 1970s and 1980s, as the economy shifted toward capital-intensive industries like steel, electronics, shipbuilding and chemicals, secondary education expanded significantly. By the 1990s and beyond, as Korea entered the era of high technology, the growth of tertiary education supported the development of advanced industries such as semiconductors, automobiles, information and communication technology (ICT) and biotechnology (BT). In this way, the expansion of education consistently paralleled Korea's stages of industrial development.

Vocational education also played a central role in this process. In 1967, vocational training was formally integrated into the public education system. The government established numerous vocational high schools across the country, specializing in fields such as mechanics, electronics, railway operations, communications, agriculture and accounting. These schools offered free or low-cost education and were regarded among the top secondary institutions. Graduates were highly sought after by companies, exempted from the mandatory three-year military service and often given preferential admission to universities. General high schools also offered vocational tracks for students seeking direct employment after graduation.

In 1965, the government encouraged colleges and universities to expand enrollment in engineering and science-related disciplines. To achieve this, it imposed quotas requiring universities to maintain a higher proportion of students in science and technology majors than in liberal arts. By 1968, the number of science majors exceeded those in liberal arts. These graduates became essential contributors to Korea's industrialization. Furthermore, in 1976, the government enacted a law requiring employers to provide compulsory vocational training, enabling many workers to receive further technical education while employed.

As discussed earlier, education played a vital role in transforming Korea's large population into a productive labor force.[10] At the same time, the labor market functioned efficiently, channeling workers into industries that needed them most. Men and women from rural areas migrated en masse to urban centers, finding employment in factories or domestic work. This labor mobility helped sustain industrial expansion, as there were few barriers in the labor market. Labor unions were weak, and no minimum wage system existed at the time.

Although the Labor Standards Act of 1953 set a legal limit of 8 working hours per day and 48 per week, actual working hours were much longer, reaching an average of 56 hours by 1982.[11] Korean workers consistently recorded some of the longest working hours in the world, a pattern that continues to appear in international surveys. While their productivity initially lagged behind that of workers in advanced countries, their strong work ethic and endurance compensated for this gap. Many have said that Korea's remarkable economic growth was built on the sacrifice of its workers. Economist Andrew Salman once remarked that "Korea's labor was the muscle that built the miracle".[12]

In the late 1960s, Korea also made deliberate efforts to bring home skilled professionals who had studied and worked abroad, particularly scientists and engineers trained in the US. A key part of this strategy was the establishment of the Korea Institute of Science and Technology (KIST) in 1966. KIST served two purposes. It was both a research institution to develop and disseminate advanced technologies to Korean industries and an attractive platform for drawing Korean scientists and engineers back from overseas by offering competitive salaries and well-equipped research facilities. This initiative helped strengthen Korea's technological foundation and fostered the human capital necessary for sustained industrial and technological progress.

3.4 Savings and investment, leading to capital accumulation

3.4.1 Korean college-graduate miners in West Germany

On December 8, 1964, President Park boarded a plane arranged by West Germany for an official visit that would prove critical for both his leadership and South Korea's economy. At that time, South Korea was facing a severe shortage of foreign currency. Following Park's military coup on May 16, 1961, the US suspended financial support in protest of his illegitimate seizure of power. The visit to West Germany was therefore a desperate but decisive step to secure much-needed funding. During the trip, President Park successfully negotiated a commercial loan of 150 million Deutsche Marks (approximately $30 million). According to an unofficial account, West Germany accepted the loan deal with the earnings of Korean miners and nurses working in West Germany held as collateral. This agreement allowed Korea to narrowly avert a looming foreign exchange crisis.

Korea began sending workers to West Germany in 1963, starting with 5,000 miners and 2,000 nurses. Jobs were scarce at home, and thus, the opportunity to work abroad attracted an overwhelming number of applicants. For the 5,000 miner positions, more than 50,000 people applied, many of whom were college graduates. By 1977, a total of 7,932 miners and 10,226 nurses had worked in West Germany. Their employment contracts typically lasted three years, during which they remitted between 70% and 90% of their monthly earnings, averaging $100 to their families in Korea. During his visit, President Park traveled to a coal mine in the Ruhr region with West German President *Heinrich Lübke* to meet 500 Korean miners. Standing before them, he encouraged, "Let's work hard and make Korea a prosperous country". The moment was deeply emotional, and all miners wept as they sang the Korean national anthem with President Park.

In addition to earnings from workers in West Germany, the Korean government secured foreign currency during two other critical moments: its participation in the Vietnam War and the normalization of diplomatic relations with Japan. Between 1965 and 1973, South Korea dispatched 312,853 soldiers to Vietnam. In return, it received $680 million in economic aid and business contracts from the US during 1966–1970. These funds were instrumental in financing major infrastructure projects, including the construction of the Seoul–Busan Expressway, a landmark achievement that later became vital to Korea's rapid industrialization.

The normalization of diplomatic ties with Japan in 1965 was another milestone in Korea's effort to secure development funds. President Park's government had proposed building a national steel plant. This project was later turned into POSCO, now one of the world's largest steel producers. Initially, the International Bank for Reconstruction and Development (IBRD) rejected Korea's request for financing, deeming the project financially unfeasible. When attempts to attract private funding from US companies also failed, President Park turned to Japan. After 14 years of negotiation, the Korea–Japan Normalization Treaty was signed on June 22, 1965, providing Korea with $800 million in grants and loans.[13] Despite widespread public opposition, Park pressed ahead with the agreement, using the funds to establish POSCO which proved pivotal in Korea's industrial transformation.

After liberation in 1945, Korea received two main types of foreign aid: project assistance and non-project assistance. Non-project aid primarily consisted of essential goods such as flour, sugar and energy supplies, while project aid focused on building infrastructure and manufacturing capacity. However, most foreign assistance during the early years was non-project-based. For instance, under US International Cooperation Administration (ICA) aid, only 27% of assistance went toward infrastructure and industrial development. US grants after the Korean War were exceptional in that they were used to rebuild key infrastructure such as roads, bridges and railways. The lack of sufficient project-based aid was one reason why Korean professionals—miners, nurses and engineers—were encouraged to work abroad to earn foreign currency.

During Korea's economic take-off, foreign aid remained the primary source of external finance. Between 1965 and 1974, foreign aid accounted for 42% of total fixed capital formation. The Korean government's foremost priority in the 1960s and 1970s was to secure and efficiently allocate foreign currency to accelerate industrialization. By law, all foreign exchange earnings were channeled into designated banks and then distributed strategically to import raw materials, fund export-oriented industries and finance large-scale infrastructure projects. A significant portion of these funds also went directly to private companies investing in plant construction and equipment for export industries. Through such disciplined management of scarce foreign capital, Korea was able to lay the financial groundwork for its industrial and economic transformation.

3.4.2 Entrepreneurial risk-taking

In most developing countries, savings are scarce, and Korea was no exception in its early years of development. Before the onset of rapid economic growth, Korea's investment rate stood at 10.9% of GDP in 1960, while its domestic savings rate was only 0.8% of GDP. During 1963–1966, investment and savings rose to average levels of 15.3% and 9.2%, respectively. However, the gap between them persisted even after the initial take-off phase.

Because the financial system was underdeveloped, entrepreneurs could not rely on formal banking institutions for capital. Instead, they depended on personal savings and loans from relatives and friends and retained earnings from their own businesses. Most of profits were not used for personal consumption but were reinvested into business expansion, acquisition of machinery and technological improvement. This pattern of reinvestment allowed firms to grow steadily and created a culture of capital accumulation that became the backbone of Korea's rapid economic growth. By prioritizing long-term reinvestment over short-term profit, businessmen played a central role in building the foundation of the nation's industrialization.

Korean entrepreneurs demonstrated an exceptional degree of courage, initiative and optimism, reflecting what economist *John Maynard Keynes* described as 'animal spirits'. This entrepreneurial drive was evident in their willingness to undertake substantial risks despite limited experience and scarce resources. They embarked on projects that were widely regarded as unattainable at the time. Large shipyards were constructed, a steel industry was developed despite skepticism from international lenders and automobiles were manufactured for export despite the absence of prior experience in car production. Their determination, vision and perseverance translated government policies into concrete industrial achievements. This entrepreneurial dynamism also extended beyond Korea's borders. During the 1970s, many Korean firms actively participated in construction projects in the Middle East and established production networks overseas.

Business leaders such as *Chung Ju-yung* (1915–2001), *Lee Byung-chul* (1910–1987), *Park Tae-joon* (1927–2011) and *Kim Woo-jung* (1936–2019) were a few among many visionary entrepreneurs. *Chung Ju-yung*, the founder of Hyundai, began with a small construction company and later expanded into shipbuilding, automobiles and heavy industries. Despite the lack of experience and technology, he took the bold step of establishing a shipyard and successfully launched Korea's shipbuilding industry. *Lee Byung-chul*, the founder of Samsung, transformed his trading business into a diversified industrial conglomerate, investing heavily in electronics, chemicals and machinery, which became the foundation for Korea's export-led growth. *Park Tae-joon* established POSCO, Korea's first integrated steel mill, despite widespread skepticism, and supplied essential materials for industrialization. *Kim Woo-jung*, the founder of Daewoo, expanded Korea's presence overseas through global trade, manufacturing and construction projects in countries such as Vietnam, Iran, India and Libya.

While the government provided the strategic vision and policy framework, it was the determination, innovation and risk-taking of entrepreneurs that translated developmental aspirations into tangible outcomes. Entrepreneurs assumed substantial risks, reinvested profits and expanded production capacity. The combination of disciplined saving and bold investment generated a virtuous cycle that supported Korea's rapid economic transformation. Savings supplied the financial resources necessary for industrialization, while entrepreneurial dynamism ensured that capital was allocated productively and strategically. The willingness of business leaders to reinvest earnings, adopt new technologies and pursue long-term objectives contributed to industrial expansion and enhanced productivity across sectors.

Notes

1 Korea unified old three states within its current borders for the first time in the 17th century, and except for invasions by Mongols and Japanese and direct Japanese colonial rule from 1905 (formally from 1910), through 1945 it was governed by Koreans as a unified state, until its division by the allied powers at the end of World War II in 1945, after which it was self-governing as two separate states.

2 Il SaKong and Youngsun Koh, *The Korean Economy*, 2010, KDI.

3 The Farmland Reform Act of 1949 prohibited non-farmers from owning land and banned tenancy farming. While compensation to landlords and sales to farmers

were both below market prices, the reform upheld the principle of compensated transfer. Before the reform, only 35% of farmland was cultivated by owner-farmers; afterward, the figure rose to 96%.

4 The gap was financed mainly by aids from the US.

5 As Korea's export earnings grew and liberalization continued, average tariffs declined to 23.7% in 1982 and to 7.9% in 1994.

6 The Rhee's government was dismantled by democratic movement by students on April 19, 1960, and Jang's government came into office. The new government revised the Seven-Year Plan and announced five-year economic development plan in 1961. Again, just one day after the announcement of the plan, military coup dismantled Jang's government, and thus, the plan had no chance for being implemented.

7 Il SaKong and Youngsun Koh, *The Korean Economy*, 2010, KDI, p16.

8 Il SaKong and Youngsun Koh, *The Korean Economy*, 2010, KDI, p229.

9 The first baby boom generation (1955–1963) built the foundation of modern Korea through industrial labor and economic development, and the second baby boom generation (1968–1974) advanced it into the era of democratization and globalization.

10 In Korea, 1955–1960 was the baby boom which recorded the highest annual population growth rate of 3.1%.

11 Minimum wage system, as imperfect form, was introduced in 1988 and its coverage was gradually expanded thereafter in Korea.

12 Andrew Salman, *The Korea Times*, from rags to riches, 2010. 4. 2

13 Total amount consisted of grant ($300 million), official loan ($200 million) and commercial loan ($300 million).

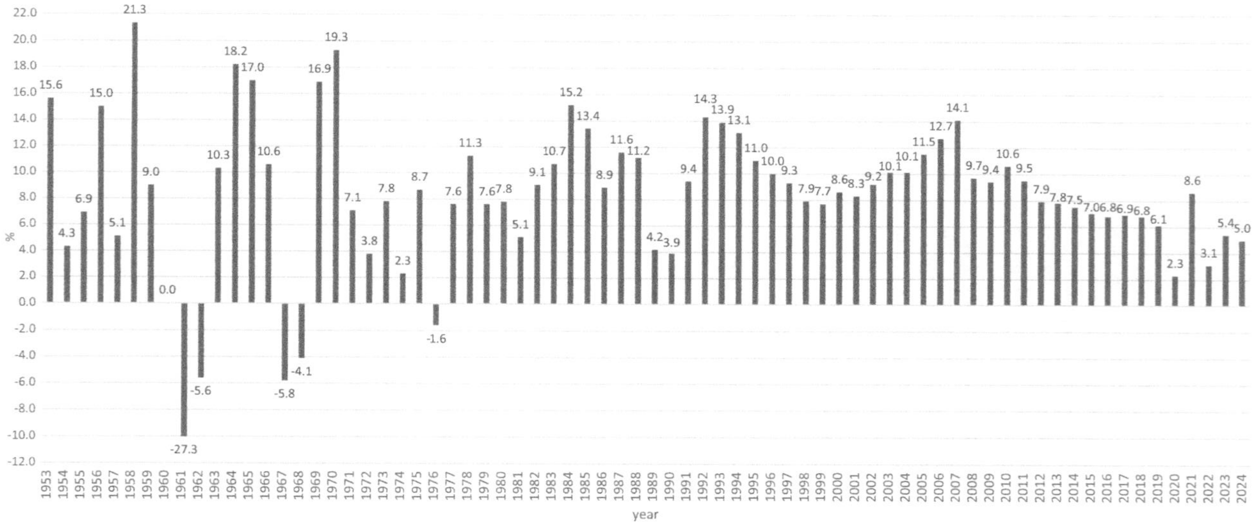

Figure 3 China's GDP growth rate (1953–2024).

Sources: GDP growth rates for 1961–2024 are drawn from the World Bank's *World Development Indicators*. Data for the period prior to 1961 are compiled from various domestic statistical sources.

4 China, 'Ascension of Dragon'

China is now the world's second largest economy after the US and the largest exporter. It surpassed Japan in total GDP in 2010, effectively joining the 'G2'. By 2016, its share of global exports was about 11.8%, ahead of the US. Rapid growth in exports and large inflows of foreign direct investment (FDI) transformed China into the 'world's factory'. It also holds the world's largest foreign exchange reserves, which at their peak were roughly $4 trillion.[1]

Half a century ago, the outlook was far less promising. In the first half of the 20th century, China's economy expanded only marginally. After the founding of the People's Republic in 1949, per capita income growth remained modest about 2.7% annually in 1961–1970 and 4.3% in 1971–1980. The Great Leap Forward and the subsequent famine of 1959–1961 caused catastrophic loss of life, and the Cultural Revolution (1966–1976) further set the country back. On the eve of reform, per capita income remained among the lowest in the world, under $100.

The turning point came in 1978, when *Deng Xiaoping* launched a program of 'reform and opening'. After his visits to the US, Japan and Southeast Asia in 1979, China moved to open its economy to trade and foreign investment. Over the next three decades, real GDP grew at close to 10% per year on average, producing an extraordinary rise in living standards and the most rapid poverty reduction in history. At the start of reform, more than 60% of the population lived below one-dollar-a-day (PPP) poverty line. By 2004, that share had fallen to about 10%, implying that roughly half a billion people exited extreme poverty within a generation. Per capita GDP grew by about 8.2% annually in the 1980s, 9.2% in the 1990s and 2000s and 6.9% in 2011–2018.

China's rise astonished the world for two main reasons, creating far greater surprise and impact than the earlier rise of Japan or the Asian Tigers. First, the scale of its transformation was unprecedented. Success in the world's most populous nation produced far-reaching global consequences. Second, China accomplished this remarkable growth while preserving a political system fundamentally different from those of advanced Western economies. *Deng Xiaoping* described this model as a 'socialist market economy', and successive leaders continued to balance a highly centralized political structure with an increasingly decentralized and market-oriented economic system.

DOI: 10.4324/9781003797135-4

It is clear what constrained China's growth and dynamism before 1978. Among the key factors were rigid central planning, collectivized production, the lack of private enterprise and market competition, economic isolation and frequent political upheavals. The market-oriented reforms and external opening that began in 1979 largely explain the subsequent acceleration of growth. Over time, high domestic investment, a well-educated labor force and integration into global value chains sustained China's remarkable long-term economic expansion, along with institutional reforms and pragmatic policymaking.

At first glance, China's extraordinary three decades of expansion might seem like a familiar story, a replay of the government-led, export-driven, FDI-fueled growth model pioneered by Japan and the Asian Tigers. But a closer look reveals that China's ascent is far more audacious and complex. When reform began, China was not merely behind. It was starting from the shadows. The economy lacked a functioning market system, enforceable property rights or meaningful exposure to global standards. Almost every productive asset was in the hands of the state, and private enterprise was little more than an experiment whispered on the margins of policy debate.

Despite all the high hurdles, China ignited one of the most spectacular economic transformations in modern history. Factories multiplied, cities rose from the dust and a billion people were lifted from poverty, all within a single lifetime. However, beneath this triumph lies a deeper tension. The same state-led structure risks constraining its next leap forward. State-owned enterprises (SOEs) remain bloated and inefficient. Financial markets are underdeveloped. Income inequality deepens across the vast social landscape.

Today, China stands at a new crossroads. Strategic rivalry with the US has reshaped the landscape of globalization, turning open economic competition into a struggle for technological dominance. Many countries no longer view China as a developing economy in need of guidance, while simultaneously pressuring it to adhere to advanced international standards. The challenges China now faces differ fundamentally from those of the early reform era, and the nation can no longer simply replicate the development paths once followed by its Asian neighbors.

4.1 Free and open market economy

4.1.1 A hybrid of market system

China began its economic development from a markedly different starting point than most other Asian economies and followed a distinctive path toward transformation. There were fundamental differences in the ways markets developed and openness to the global economy evolved. Following the Soviet model, market forces initially played only a minor role in China's economy. Industrial inputs and most outputs were allocated through government directives and SOEs. Essential consumer goods, including food, clothing and household necessities, were distributed through a rationing system based on coupons. 'Who got What' was decided by the central planning system of the State Planning Commission.

Prior to the economic reforms initiated in 1978, China undertook several efforts to promote national development. Among them, *the Great Leap Forward* (1958–1961) and *the Cultural Revolution* (1966–1976) were the most ambitious in scale. The Great Leap Forward, which formed part of the Second Five-Year Plan, set ambitious targets such as rapidly expanding steel production, with the aim of doubling output within a year and catching up with Britain within 15 years. However, these objectives proved unrealistic in the absence of sufficient investment, technological capacity and managerial expertise.

The Cultural Revolution, while primarily a political movement, also had serious economic consequences. Both initiatives ultimately failed to deliver economic growth or prosperity, even though some progress was made in public health and rural development. These efforts faltered because they attempted to achieve economic advancement through ideology rather than through technological innovation, capital accumulation and proper incentives. Leaders at the time overestimated the power of mass enthusiasm and collective effort to generate productivity without modern technology and system.

Before 1978, approximately 80% of China's population were peasants living in rural areas and working in communes. Communal land was collectively owned, and peasants were compensated based on overall commune output rather than individual effort. Since farmers did not benefit directly from their additional labor or investment, productivity remained low. The collective agricultural system failed to generate sufficient food or income for the population.

China's transformation began in 1978 with the introduction of the 'household responsibility system'. This reform dismantled the communal structure and allocated land-use rights to individual households, allowing them to retain the output from their own plots. This system created strong incentives for productivity, leading to dramatic gains in agricultural output. Grain production increased from 305 million tons in 1978 to 407 million tons in 1984 after the transition to household-based farming.

The success of rural reform gave the Chinese leadership confidence to pursue broader changes. Ownership of land in China, however, remained fundamentally different from that in other Asian economies. As *Joe Studwell* observed, "A Chinese peasant does not own his or her land". When land was divided among households in 1979, the government intentionally avoided creating private property rights. A series of land laws extended the duration of farmers' land-use contracts, with each household typically cultivating an average plot of about one-third of a hectare. The Land Administration Law of 1998 established 30-year contracts for land use, maintaining state ownership but granting secure and transferable use rights to farmers. These rights were later reinforced by the Property Law in 2007, which recognized farmers' land-use rights as functionally equivalent to private property. These reforms, combined with higher procurement prices for agricultural products, unleashed strong incentives for increased production and rural prosperity.

In the industrial sector, the introduction of private ownership proceeded more slowly, gradually and incompletely than in the agricultural sector. The Chinese government continued to support SOEs, particularly those producing intermediate goods, while firms manufacturing consumer goods received little direct assistance. However, the rise of township and village enterprises (TVEs)[2] represented a critical step toward a market-oriented economy. TVEs were hybrid institutions that blended elements of socialism and capitalism, combining local government ownership with market-based operations.

TVEs thrived because they operated flexibly within China's weak legal and institutional framework, where formal markets and contract enforcement were still underdeveloped. Their success stemmed from pragmatic experimentation, innovation and adaptation to local conditions. This eclectic approach proved highly effective, laying the groundwork for China's later industrialization and export expansion. Over the following decades, market incentives, entrepreneurial initiative and global integration propelled China's rapid growth. These forces lifted hundreds of millions of people out of poverty. They also established China as a leading example of how gradual market reforms within a socialist framework can bring about economic transformation.[3]

Interestingly, these transformations did not originate as a Communist Party directive but rather emerged from local innovation. The best-known example of this kind originated in Xiaogang Village in Anhui Province in 1978. At that time, agricultural production in China operated under the People's Commune system.[4] This arrangement provided little incentive for individuals to work hard. In response, 18 farmers in Xiaogang village secretly signed an agreement to divide the commune's land among households. Each family would cultivate its own plot, deliver a fixed quota of grain to the state and keep or sell the surplus. The results were immediate and striking. Grain output more than doubled within a year, and food shortages in the village were effectively eliminated. The success of the experiment led to its rapid spread. Indeed, as *Deng Xiaoping* later acknowledged, "It was the peasants who invented the household contract responsibility system with remuneration linked to output".

4.1.2 Zheng Hee's last exploration in 1434

The year 1434 marks a pivotal moment in Chinese history, the beginning of the maritime closure policy under *the Ming dynasty* (1368–1644). The emperor decided to end ocean voyages and prohibit international maritime trade to reduce the immense costs of naval expeditions and to concentrate resources on defending China's northern border. This decision led to the dismantling of what had been the world's largest and most advanced fleet. Before this closure, Admiral *Zheng Hee* had led grand expeditions across the Indian Ocean, reaching as far as the east coast of Africa and spreading Chinese culture, knowledge and influence. The emperor's choice to terminate maritime trade and shut down shipyards effectively removed China from global exploration and commerce, isolating it from international exchange.

Following the imposition of the maritime ban, overseas trade was tightly restricted for several centuries, and China adopted an inward-looking policy that contributed to prolonged economic isolation. This decision was made at a critical historical juncture, as global long-distance trade began to expand rapidly during the late 14th and early 15th centuries. By turning inward, China gradually lost its early advantages in technology and productivity. Once the most prosperous nation in the world, it experienced stagnation while Western countries continued to advance.

China's long-standing policy of isolation did not end through internal reform but through external pressure from Western powers. In the 19th century, European nations sought new markets for their goods, and Britain initiated *the Opium Wars* (1839–1842, 1856–1860) to force open Chinese ports. Even after its defeat, China remained reluctant to open its economy and continued to maintain strict control over foreign trade. In contrast to Japan's Meiji Restoration which embraced industrialization and modernization, China's *Qing Dynasty* (1644–1912) was reluctant to adopt outward-looking policies. Although *the Self-Strengthening Movement* (1861–1895) attempted to import Western technologies and establish modern state-owned industries, these efforts were limited and fragmented. The reforms failed to halt the decline of *the Qing dynasty*.[5]

The policy of isolation persisted through prolonged periods of domestic conflict and political upheaval, as the government continued to restrict external engagement and prioritize internal stability over international economic interaction. The tide turned in 1978 when *Deng Xiaoping* launched the Reform and Opening-Up policy.[6] Trade and FDI became central to China's economic strategy. The government replaced administrative controls on imports and exports with tariffs, quotas and licenses, later phasing out most restrictions. In 2001, China joined the World Trade Organization (WTO), marking full integration into the global trading system. The share of exports and imports in GDP rose dramatically from 10% in 1978 to 33% in 1990, 49% in 2002 and 67% in 2006. Export expansion became the primary engine of China's rapid economic growth.[7]

FDI played an equally vital role. It provided not only capital but also advanced technologies, managerial expertise and higher production standards. From 1984 to 1993, FDI inflows grew at an average annual rate of 40.9%, increasing from $1.26 billion to $27.6 billion. By 1993, foreign capital accounted for 7.3% of total domestic capital formation. Between 2000 and 2011, annual FDI averaged around $77 billion, making China the largest recipient of foreign investment among developing countries. The government's flexible, strategic policies ensured that foreign investment aligned with national development goals.

To maximize the benefits of FDI, the Chinese government encouraged technology transfer, local partnerships and export-oriented production. The centerpiece of its outward-opening strategy was the creation of special economic zones (SEZs). These zones served as controlled environments in which market principles could be tested without challenging the broader political system. The SEZs allowed China to attract foreign investment while managing the risks of liberalization.

In 1980, four coastal cities such as Shenzhen, Xiamen, Shantou and Zhuhai were designated as the first SEZs. They were followed by 14 additional coastal cities in 1984 and later by entire regions such as the Yangtze River Delta, the Pearl River Delta and the Minnan area. SEZs also became laboratories for joint ventures between foreign investors and SOEs, especially in Guangdong and Fujian provinces. The success of SEZs was extraordinary. By 2007, they accounted for 22% of China's GDP, 46% of total FDI and 60% of exports, while generating approximately 30 million jobs. SEZs symbolized China's re-entry into the global economy, transforming the nation from a closed, centrally planned system into one of the world's most dynamic and outward-oriented economies.

4.2 Accountable government and effective policies

4.2.1 Visionary leadership

In China, the strong leadership of the state played a decisive role in achieving rapid economic growth. Visionary and reform-minded leader *Deng Xiaoping* (1904–1997) provided long-term direction and a clear vision for the country's economic and social transformation. Under his guidance, capable and disciplined bureaucrats implemented these visions through systematic development planning, targeted industrial policies and effective execution.

The Chinese leadership drew valuable lessons from its earlier mistakes. The Cultural Revolution (1966–1976) was primarily a political upheaval that caused severe disruption to the economy. Government economic agencies were paralyzed, planning and coordination broke down and factory management was taken over by revolutionary committees that lacked technical and managerial expertise. Market mechanisms were abolished, and private production was prohibited in both rural and urban areas. As a result, China's economy became isolated from global markets and foreign technology, stifling growth and innovation.

Following the downfall of *the Gang of Four* in 1976,[8] a new generation of leaders, headed by long-time reformist *Deng Xiaoping*, initiated a comprehensive program of market-oriented reform and opening-up. At the historic 'Third Plenary Session of the 11th Central Committee' in December 1978, the Chinese Communist Party decided to set ideology aside and prioritize economic development. Deng placed practical results above ideological rigidity. His famous saying, "It doesn't matter whether a cat is black or white, as long as it catches mice.", reflected his belief that what mattered most was effectiveness, not adherence to dogma. He argued that socialism could accommodate market reforms if they contributed to economic growth and national strength.

During his visit to Japan in October 1978, *Deng Xiaoping* was deeply impressed by the Shinkansen high-speed railway and Panasonic's advanced color television production lines, prompting his famous remark that China really needs to run to catch up. A central component of his vision was the 'Four Modernizations', which referred to the modernization of agriculture, industry, national defense and science and technology. Deng regarded these as essential areas for revitalizing China and enabling it to recover from decades of economic stagnation.

The reforms that followed were gradual, pragmatic and experimental. As Deng famously remarked, "China would cross the river by feeling the stones". This approach stood in sharp contrast to the 'shock therapy' reforms later pursued in the Soviet Union and Eastern European countries. Reform began in rural areas through local experimentation. The introduction of the household responsibility system in several provinces allowed farmers to manage their own plots and sell surplus output at market prices. This arrangement significantly improved agricultural productivity and rural incomes while reducing poverty. After proving successful, it was adopted nationwide, effectively dismantling the commune system and restoring incentives for individual production.

The leadership pursued reform cautiously, introducing what became known as 'the dual-track system'.[9] This strategy allowed for gradual liberalization while maintaining stability. Under the dual-track system, goods and production within the state plan continued to be traded at fixed prices, while production beyond the plan could be sold at market-determined prices. This approach enabled private enterprises to respond to supply and demand without dismantling the existing planning structure overnight. The dual-track system remained in place until the early 1990s, allowing the economy to adjust smoothly.

4.2.2 Reforming SOEs

Before the launch of reform and opening in 1978, China's manufacturing sector was relatively underdeveloped and played only a limited role in the national economy. Manufacturing accounted for just 12.5% of national income. Mining and heavy industries were concentrated mainly in the northeastern provinces, while light industries were located primarily in coastal cities such as Shanghai and Tianjin. The Chinese leadership sought to modernize the economy through socialist industrialization, adopting a Soviet-style centrally planned economy based on public ownership of the means of production.

The State Planning Commission directed national economic planning. Under the First Five-Year Plan (1953–1957), the Chinese government implemented approximately 1,000 large-scale investment projects aimed at developing heavy industry, many of which received technical and financial support from the Soviet Union. This socialist transformation brought nearly all industrial and commercial enterprises under state ownership. By the end of the plan, more than 90% of handicraft producers and household farms had been reorganized into cooperatives under collective ownership.

After the launch of the reform in 1978, the transformation of SOEs became one of the most important and challenging aspects of China's transition from a centrally planned economy to what is now known as a 'socialist market economy'. The Chinese government recognized that SOEs, which had been the backbone of the command economy, suffered from inefficiency, overstaffing and outdated management systems. The goal of reform was therefore not only to make these enterprises more productive and profitable but also to redefine their role in a more market-oriented economic structure.

The transformation of SOEs took place in several stages. In the late 1970s and 1980s, the government began by granting SOEs greater operational autonomy while maintaining state ownership. Enterprises were allowed to retain part of their profits, make limited decisions about production and pricing and reward employees based on performance. In the 1990s, China entered a deeper phase of reform aimed at corporatization and market orientation. The government sought to separate administrative control from enterprise management and turn SOEs into independent, market-driven corporations. From the 2000s onward, the government's focus shifted toward strategic consolidation. The state aimed to strengthen large SOEs operating in critical sectors while continuing to merge, privatize or close smaller ones.

The reform approach differed between small and large SOEs. This differentiated strategy, encapsulated by the policy of 'grasping the large, letting go of the small', enabled China to combine market dynamism with state control. Small SOEs, especially those in consumer goods and local services, were privatized or merged to improve efficiency and reduce the government's financial burden. Privatization and deregulation were the main approaches. Many medium and small enterprises were sold to private owners, while others were granted greater operational autonomy.

Large SOEs in strategic industries were corporatized, consolidated and strengthened under continued state ownership, becoming the pillars of China's industrial and technological ambitions. The government restructured operations and introduced competition among firms that had previously enjoyed monopolistic power. This restructuring covered vital industries such as oil and gas, petrochemicals, coal, electricity, telecommunications, banking and insurance. Exposed to both domestic competition and international competition, these enterprises adopted global standards, improved productivity and in some cases became world-class producers, particularly in sectors such as hydropower and high-speed rail.

Unlike Japan and Korea, where private companies primarily drove technology acquisition and innovation, the Chinese government itself played a direct role in facilitating technology transfer. The National Development and Reform Commission (NDRC), the key agency responsible for industrial planning and coordination, took the role of technology transfer from foreign companies. In exchange for access to China's vast domestic market, foreign multinational corporations were required to share advanced technologies with local partners. For instance, the government arranged for Westinghouse, a US power company, to transfer thermal turbine technology to Chinese state-owned engineering firms. Siemens was forced to provide hydropower turbine technology to domestic manufacturers. These initiatives helped Chinese SOEs build technological capabilities, later enhanced through overseas projects in countries such as India and Venezuela.[10]

By 2010, SOEs accounted for only about 4% of all enterprises in terms of number. Nevertheless, they continued to play a significant role in the industrial sector, contributing roughly 25% of industrial value added, controlling around 48% of industrial assets and employing about 18% of the industrial labor force. Most of the remaining SOEs were large corporations, and many of them listed on stock exchanges but majority owned by the state and concentrated in strategic sectors such as energy, transportation, finance and telecommunications. The State-Owned Assets Supervision and Administration Commission (SASAC), established in 2003, was tasked with managing these enterprises. At its inception, SASAC oversaw 196 major central state-owned groups, and this number was gradually reduced through consolidation in the following years.

4.3 Education and human resource development

4.3.1 The cultural revolution broadened rural education

Since the founding of the People's Republic of China in 1949, human capital development has consistently been a top national priority. The government has continuously adjusted its education policies to match different stages of economic development, with the goal of improving the skills and literacy of the entire population. During the 1950s and 1960s, the main objective was eradicating illiteracy, making universal primary education the first national goal. The government launched mass literacy campaigns and introduced simplified Chinese characters to make reading and writing more accessible to the population.

In 1966, there was a dramatic reversion in education policy. Chairman *Mao Zedong* (1893–1976) launched *the Cultural Revolution*, a radical political movement that profoundly disrupted China's society, economy and education system. One of the most significant consequences of this upheaval was the collapse of formal education during 1966–1976. Mao's education policies were deeply rooted in his radical egalitarian ideals, which sought to eliminate class distinctions and promote socialist values. However, these policies severely hindered the accumulation of human capital among the affected generations, creating long-lasting gaps in education and skills development.

In December 1968, Mao issued an important directive that became known as the 'send-down movement'. His statement declared, "It is very necessary for the urban educated youth to go to the countryside to be re-educated by poor farmers". This policy required approximately 16 million urban youth, mostly junior and senior high school graduates, to relocate to rural areas, where they remained until the late 1970s. While many of these young people were expected to engage in agricultural labor, a significant number were assigned to teach rural children due to their higher educational background. Unexpectedly, this policy expanded educational access for about 245 million rural school-age children, even though it deprived the urban youth themselves of further formal education.

The Cultural Revolution also served as a social equalizer in educational access. One of its most symbolic reforms was the abolition of entrance examinations, which had long been a cornerstone of the Chinese education system. Education during this period shifted its focus toward the working class and peasantry, while higher education received far less attention. Before the Cultural Revolution, children's educational attainment closely reflected that of their parents, reinforcing social stratification. Afterward, this correlation weakened considerably, indicating a partial leveling effect, though achieved at great social and economic cost.

China's education system began to recover only after 1977, when universities reopened and entrance examinations were reinstated. The results were remarkable. Illiteracy among young and middle-aged peasants fell from 80% in 1949 to 30% by the early 1980s after four rounds of literacy campaigns. Enrollment in primary education rose from 68.2% in 1970 to 100% in 2005, while secondary education increased from 23.5% to 76.0% over the same period. Tertiary education expanded from a mere 0.9% in 1970 to 22.0% in 2005. Consequently, the share of the population aged 15–24 with no schooling dropped dramatically from 16.3% in 1970 to just 0.1% in 2010.

It is a common misconception that the Chinese government alone drove its educational and human resource development. Individuals, families and private enterprises have played an essential role in advancing human capital. Education has been deeply embedded in Chinese culture since the time of Confucius, who regarded learning as the foundation of moral cultivation and social advancement.[11] This cultural tradition encouraged families to make substantial investments in education, viewing it as the most reliable path to social mobility and prosperity. During the imperial era, basic education was often organized through home-based schools, where wealthy families or communities hired scholars to teach local children.

In modern China, this tradition continues. The private tutoring industry has grown rapidly since the 1980s, becoming a multibillion business, much like in Japan and Korea. The fierce competition for university entrance examinations has driven many students to enroll in private academies for supplemental study, often at significant cost. Education remains the principal means for individuals to advance socially and economically, a legacy of the imperial examination system that historically determined civil service appointments. This enduring respect for education has fostered a culture of continuous learning and aspiration, contributing to China's substantial human capital development and supplying the skilled workforce that underpins its economic success.

4.3.2 Family planning and demographic change

During China's economic take-off, the country's high fertility rate initially posed a significant obstacle to growth rather than a demographic advantage. In 1960, China's total fertility rate was 6.2, rising slightly to 6.3 by 1965. Recognizing that rapid population growth could hinder economic development, the government launched a nationwide family planning campaign in the early 1970s. The campaign promoted three principles: having fewer children, marrying later and spacing births at intervals of at least three years. This approach later evolved into the well-known one-child policy introduced in 1979.

As a result, the birth rate fell dramatically from 4.9 in 1970 to 3.0 in 1975, 2.5 in 1980 and 1.8 in 1990. Lower fertility reduced the dependency ratio, freeing more parents from child-rearing responsibilities and allowing greater participation in the labor force. A smaller dependency burden also boosted household savings. Together, these effects contributed to China's rapid economic take-off by expanding the workforce and increasing investment capacity. By 2010, the total fertility rate had fallen further to 1.4, driven not only by strict birth control policies but also by rising female education levels and higher wages.

The demographic transformation yielded what economists call a 'demographic dividend'. As birth rates declined, the working-age population (aged 15–64) surged from about 625 million in the early 1980s to 1 billion in 2014. The proportion of working-age individuals in the total population rose from 62% in the early 1980s to 75% in 2010. This shift significantly raised per capita GDP, as a greater share of the population became economically productive.[12]

Labor mobility also played a vital role in sustaining economic growth. One of the most influential institutions affecting labor movement in China was the household registration system (*Hukou*), introduced in 1958. Initially designed to control population distribution under socialist planning, the Hukou system tied individuals' residency and occupational rights to their place of birth. Nearly all aspects of life, including land allocation, housing, education, healthcare and social security, depended on one's Hukou status. For example, children could attend public schools only within the jurisdiction of their registered household.

The Hukou system effectively divided China's labor force into two groups, urban workers and rural workers. Urban Hukou holders enjoyed better access to education, healthcare and employment, while rural residents were confined to agricultural work and restricted from freely moving to cities. As a result, during the 1950s through the 1980s, China's urban population remained at only 15%–18% of the total.

Before the reforms, employment allocation was centrally managed through government labor bureaus. Workers had little freedom to choose their jobs, and migration was heavily restricted. With the onset of the economic reforms in the late 1970s, however, it became clear that rigid labor allocation hindered productivity and growth. The government gradually replaced administrative job assignments with market-based employment mechanisms. By 1980, a more flexible labor market began to emerge. Labor bureaus transitioned from assigning workers to facilitating job matching between employers and employees. In 1986, SOEs were allowed to hire workers on short-term contracts rather than permanent appointments, increasing labor flexibility. By the mid-1990s, performance-based pay systems, bonuses and floating wages were introduced to encourage productivity.

Reforms of the Hukou system began in the early 1990s. Restrictions on mobility were gradually lifted, allowing rural residents to seek jobs in non-agricultural sectors. In 1997, migrants who had stable income or housing were permitted to obtain urban Hukou registration. These changes, combined with broader labor market reforms, greatly expanded labor mobility and enabled millions of rural workers to join the industrial and service sectors. This combination of demographic transition, rising labor participation and growing labor mobility created one of the largest and most dynamic workforces in history, fueling China's sustained industrialization and economic miracle.

Top of Form

Bottom of Form

4.4 Savings and investment, leading to capital accumulation

4.4.1 Chinese saving rate puzzle

China's exceptionally high saving rate has been a central factor underlying its sustained economic growth over the past four decades. This phenomenon reflects a combination of structural, institutional and cultural influences that encouraged households, corporations and the state to maintain unusually high levels of saving. Since the 1980s, China's gross national saving rate has consistently ranked among the highest in the world, often exceeding 40%–45% of GDP, compared with approximately 20%–25% in most advanced economies.

China's saving rate has also been notably higher than that of its Asian peers. In 1978–2008, it ranged from 34% to 53%, roughly 20% points higher than that of South Korea. The relationship between income growth and savings in China has been mutually reinforcing. Rising incomes increased the capacity to save, while high savings financed investment and further economic expansion. This virtuous cycle persisted for more than three decades. Before the reform era, the average saving rate during 1965–1977 was around 27%. By contrast, in the 2010s China's gross domestic saving rate averaged 48.3%, peaking at 53.1% in 2007, one of the highest levels recorded in modern economic history. In effect, China saved more than half of its total output, leaving a comparatively smaller share for consumption.

These savings were generated primarily by households, corporations and the government. At the outset of reform, household savings were relatively low, at around 6%–7% in 1978, largely due to limited household incomes. However, rapid income growth during the reform period enabled households to save a greater share of their earnings. Cultural traditions emphasizing thrift and financial prudence reinforced a strong propensity to save rather than spend. In addition, precautionary motives played an important role, as social safety nets for healthcare, pensions and unemployment remained limited for much of the reform era. The introduction of the one-child policy in 1979 further strengthened the incentive to save, as families anticipated reduced familial support in old age and increased the need for personal retirement resources.

Although corporations are typically viewed as investors rather than savers, Chinese firms also made a substantial contribution to national savings. Many enterprises, both state-owned and private, retained earnings rather than distributing them as dividends. This practice was partly a response to an underdeveloped financial system, which made internal financing more reliable than external borrowing. At the same time, China's investment-led growth strategy encouraged firms to accumulate capital and reinvest profits in expansion and modernization.

As a result, domestic bank loans accounted for only about 21% of total investment financing, while self-financing provided approximately 50% and rose to as much as 65% by 2008. Informal and private financing sources, particularly important for small- and medium-sized enterprises, contributed an additional 13.5%. FDI played a smaller but still meaningful role, accounting for 11.2% of total investment in 1995 before declining gradually to 2.9% in 2009.

China's high saving rate supported economic growth in several important ways. First, it enabled the country to sustain exceptionally high levels of investment, frequently exceeding 40% of GDP. These resources financed large-scale infrastructure development, industrial expansion, urban housing and technological upgrading. As a result, China was able to build the physical capital base necessary for rapid industrialization without relying heavily on external borrowing. Second, high domestic savings contributed to macroeconomic stability. Because most investment was financed internally, China largely avoided the external debt crises that affected many developing economies dependent on foreign capital. Abundant domestic savings provided a financial buffer that helped shield the economy from global shocks.

At the same time, persistently high savings, however, generated structural imbalances. The emphasis on saving restrained domestic consumption, making economic growth heavily dependent on exports and investment. Ample access to capital also contributed to overinvestment and industrial overcapacity in some sectors, reducing the efficiency of resource allocation. Internationally, China's high saving rate has been widely debated, as it has contributed to large current account surpluses while corresponding deficits have emerged in other economies.

4.4.2 A global magnet for FDI

Since economic take-off, China has consistently attracted a large share of global FDI, reflecting its position as one of the world's leading destinations for international capital. China's share of global FDI inflows increased from less than 1% in the 1980s to about 6%–8% in the 1990s and further to roughly 8%–10% in the 2000s. By 2010, annual inflows surpassed $114 billion, making China the second-largest FDI recipient in the world, after the US. In 2021, China recorded $344 billion in FDI inflows, marking one of the highest levels in its history and accounted for about 15% of global FDI inflows. Cumulatively, China's inward FDI stock[13] was estimated to reach above $3 trillion as of the end of 2024.[14] This steady rise reflected China's success in implementing market-oriented reforms, improving infrastructure and maintaining political and economic stability.

During the 1980s, China's share of global FDI inflows was very small, reflecting the early stage of its economic reform and gradual integration into the world economy. China's FDI inflows were extremely modest, and China's average share of global FDI inflows during the 1980s was estimated at less than 1% but increased sharply during the 1990s and 2000s, reflecting its successful economic liberalization, rapid industrialization and deeper integration into the global economy.

In the 1990s, China emerged as one of the most attractive destinations for foreign investors, particularly after *Deng Xiaoping*'s 'Southern Tour' in 1992,[15] which reaffirmed the country's commitment to reform and openness. As a result, FDI inflows expanded dramatically throughout the decade. By 2000, FDI inflows reached roughly $40 billion, making China the largest recipient of foreign investment among developing countries. China's share of global FDI inflows during the 1990s averaged around 6%–8%.

In the 2000s, China's role as a global investment destination grew even stronger. The country's accession to the WTO in 2001 was a turning point that accelerated liberalization, improved legal protections for investors and boosted confidence among multinational corporations. China's share of global FDI inflows in the 2000s averaged around 8%–10%. During this decade, the composition of foreign investment in China also evolved. While the 1990s had been dominated by labor-intensive manufacturing, the 2000s saw a shift toward technology-intensive industries, services and high-value sectors such as automobiles, electronics, telecommunications and finance.

The most prominent mechanism for attracting FDI was the establishment of SEZs. In 1979, as part of the new open-door policy, China designated four SEZs—Shenzhen, Zhuhai, Shantou and Xiamen—in the southeastern coastal region. Their proximity to Hong Kong facilitated strong investment flows, with roughly 80% of total FDI in these zones originating from Hong Kong investors. Between 1979 and 1983, about 80% of all FDI projects in China were concentrated within these SEZs.

Initially, the SEZs functioned as experimental laboratories for foreign investment, where special economic regulations and incentives were tested. However, their isolation from the rest of the domestic economy limited broader linkages, turning them into quasi-enclaves. To address this issue, in 1984 the government designated 14 Open Coastal Cities (OCCs), extending special policy measures beyond the SEZs. These OCCs, located across ten coastal provinces, became new centers for export-oriented industrialization and FDI absorption. Over time, the FDI inflows to the OCCs surpassed those to the original SEZs, and after 1986, foreign investment gradually spread to other coastal and inland regions.

China's openness deepened not only geographically but also institutionally. The 1979 Equity Joint Venture Law introduced only Chinese-Foreign Equity Joint Ventures (EJVs). In 1986, the government permitted the establishment of wholly foreign-owned enterprises (WFOEs), marking a significant step toward full liberalization of foreign investment. New regulations allowed foreign investors to repatriate profits freely and manage liquidation proceeds more flexibly. As restrictions were lifted, FDI inflows surged, reaching $16.8 billion annually, four times the average level of the early 1980s.

The magnitude of China's FDI inflows was unprecedented for developing economies. While many other developing economies struggled with capital shortages, China successfully attracted vast foreign investments by combining market liberalization, abundant labor and policy stability. This inflow of capital and technology not only accelerated China's industrialization but also helped integrate the country deeply into global production and trade networks, laying a foundation for its emergence as a major economic power.

Notes

1 As of mid-2025, China's foreign exchange (FX) reserves stand at about USD 3.317 trillion. The all-time peak, however, was reached in June 2014, when China's FX reserves hit approximately USD 3.993 trillion.

2 There were three types of VTEs according to the data from the Ministry of Agriculture (MOA): (a) collective TVEs, (b) privately run TVEs (larger private firms) and (c) self-employment household businesses.

3 Michael P. Todaro and Stephen C. Smith, *Economic Development*, 2015, Pearson, p200.

4 Land, tools and output were collectively owned and distributed.

5 The Xinhai Revolution of 1911 brought the fall of the Qing dynasty and the establishment of the Republic of China. Despite political instability and civil conflict, the new republic sought to promote industrial development through policies such as the introduction of patents and preferential tax systems. However, domestic industries suffered heavily from the Great Depression, the war against Japan and the subsequent civil war. Even then, the government was hesitant to open China's borders more fully.

6 When the People's Republic of China was founded in 1949, the new regime again adopted a closed-border policy that lasted nearly three decades. This isolation proved particularly damaging, as it coincided with a period of rapid expansion in global trade and economic integration elsewhere.

7 Michael H. Best, *How Growth Really Happens*, 2018, Princeton, p223.

8 The "Gang of Four" were a group of political leaders associated with the radical phase of the Cultural Revolution in China and were blamed for many of its excesses. The group consisted of Jiang Qing (Mao Zedong's wife and the most prominent member), Zhang Chunqiao, Yao Wenyuan, Wang Hongwen. They were arrested in October 1976 shortly after Mao Zedong's death. Their removal marked the end of the Cultural Revolution and opened the way for the rise of Deng Xiaoping and the subsequent program of reform.

9 Two symposiums provided momentum in adopting the system. The system was discussed at Moganshan Conference in a mountain resort in Zhejiang province in 1984 and Bashanlun Conference during a cruise on the Yangtze River in 1985. Chinese leaders finally adopted the system after intensive discussions among academics, government officials and foreign experts.

10 The mega power plants projects were financed by CDB and China Export-Import Bank.

11 The Confucian culture runs deep in the Chinese society, and education is one of the cornerstones of Confucianism. In China's imperial era, the selection of candidates for the civil service was based on examinations which tested classical studies on Confucian canons. For thousands of years, education about Confucianism had been an essential social channel for individuals to become part of the higher class.

12 Dr. Ming argued that the demographic dividend may never have existed because China's labor force as a share of the total population was roughly stable, hovering at around 50% from 1982 to 2015. *The Economist*, September 23rd–29th, 2023, p77.

13 The total value of foreign investment accumulated within the country.

14 The shares of FDI are estimated numbers, not based on strict statistics.

15 In early 1992, at the age of 87, Deng Xiaoping traveled to several southern cities including Shenzhen, Zhuhai, Guangzhou and Shanghai to reaffirm and accelerate China's reform and opening-up policy that had slowed after the political turmoil of 1989.

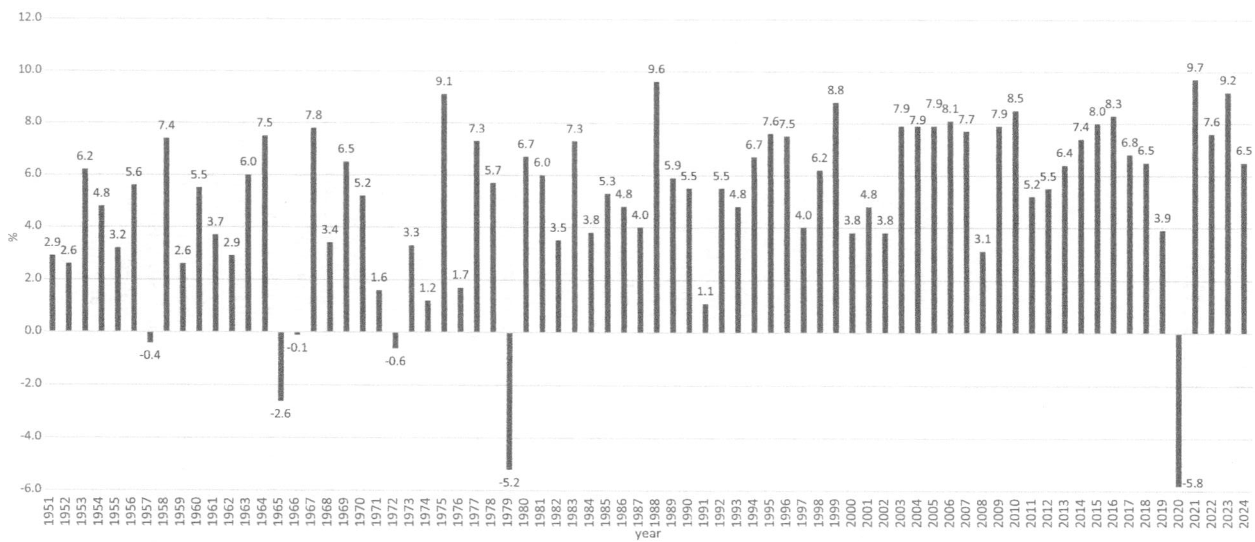

Figure 4 India's GDP growth rate (1951–2024).

Sources: GDP growth rates for 1961–2024 are drawn from the World Bank's *World Development Indicators*. Data for the period prior to 1961 are compiled from various domestic statistical sources.

5 India, 'Smart Elephant Awakens'

India's overtaking of the UK in total GDP in 2022, thereby becoming the world's fifth largest economy, was widely regarded as a symbolic milestone marking its emergence from the long shadow of colonialism. However, India's growth trajectory has differed significantly from that of its Northeast Asian counterparts, which embarked on rapid industrialization and economic expansion several decades earlier. As a relatively late entrant into sustained economic growth, India continues to face questions about whether it can maintain its current momentum over the long term, particularly in the context of a fragmented global economy increasingly characterized by nationalism, protectionism and geopolitical uncertainty.

A principal reason for India's late industrialization is its extraordinary social and economic diversity. As Jeffrey Sachs notes, India is an unmatched *mélange* of cultures and ethnicities, leadership changed frequently and policies have often shifted, lengthening deliberation and complicating execution. Each step forward typically required extended debate, negotiation and compromise so that progress has been slow or intermittent.

Historically, India possessed sophisticated industries. During *the Mughal era* (1526–1858), it was a major producer of internationally traded goods. Economic historians estimate that, around 1750, India accounted for roughly a quarter of global industrial output, with textiles as a leading export. As a result of the Industrial Revolution, European factories began producing goods at much lower costs, which flooded Indian markets and led to the onset of industrial decline in India in the late 18th century. Domestic political instability, foreign incursions and the consolidation of British rule accelerated this deindustrialization.

Economic performance improved only modestly even after independence in 1947. The 'British *Raj*' gave way to the 'License *Raj*'. The inward-looking and import-substitution strategy yielded sluggish growth. From the 1950s through the 1970s, aggregate growth averaged under 3%, the so-called 'Hindu rate of growth'. Per capita output rose by about 1.8% per year in the 1960s and only 0.6% in the 1970s. The contrast with peers was stark. In 1960, India's per capita income was roughly $90 versus Korea's $156. Then by 1990, Korea had reached about $6,600, while India had risen to only $367.

DOI: 10.4324/9781003797135-5

Despite broad reforms after independence, the core system of licenses and controls endured until the crisis of balance-of-payments in 1991. Foreign exchange reserves declined to a level sufficient to cover only about one month of imports, credit ratings were downgraded and access to international financing became increasingly constrained.

The 1991 reform program included liberalization, privatization and external opening, recasting the division of roles between state and market. The first was liberalization, which aimed to reduce government control and promote competition. The government abolished most industrial licensing, subject to a negative list, and, as a result, import licensing was sharply reduced. The second component was privatization, designed to reduce the dominance of the public sector and encourage private enterprise. Many public sector monopolies ended. The third component was globalization, which sought to integrate India more fully with the global economy. Import tariffs and quantitative restrictions were reduced, foreign direct investment (FDI) was liberalized to allow up to 51% foreign equity in many industries and automatic approval of FDI was introduced.

The results of these reforms were swift and significant. The crisis was brought under control relatively quickly, as foreign exchange reserves began to recover and inflation, which had risen to around 14% in 1991, declined to manageable levels. The GDP growth rate rebounded to an average of 5%–6% during the 1990s. As both domestic and foreign investments expanded rapidly, the economy became increasingly dynamic. The reforms transformed India to one of the world's fastest-growing emerging economies. Particularly during the 2000s, the annual growth often exceeded 7%–8%. Trade growth accelerated to more than 11% per year. Average annual FDI inflows in the 2010s were around 14 times larger than in the 1990s. Poverty rates declined significantly and the middle class expanded rapidly as annual per capita GDP growth rose to about 4.7% in 1991–2017 from roughly 2% in the 1960s–1980s.

Unlike many Asian economies that industrialized chiefly through manufacturing, India's expansion has been driven disproportionately by services, especially IT and software sectors. India started transforming its economy directly from an agricultural economy to a service sector one. India became a global center for exportable software services and IT-enabled services. The software and IT-enabled service industry today supplies about 8% of India's output and accounts for $137 billion in exports. While production and trade of goods require efficient large-scale physical infrastructure, the internet network and firm-level satellite or online connections can facilitate frequent and low-cost data transfer with duty-free. Abundant English-speaking workers could beat global competitors without decent physical infrastructure.

Even so, a demanding reform agenda remains. A central debate concerns whether India can maintain rapid growth with a services-led model. Whether a direct shift from agriculture to services can still generate mass employment and deliver productivity gains at scale remains uncertain, not least because digitally delivered services, powerful though they are, employ only a small share of the workforce.

Obviously, the Indian economy is facing two challenges for sustained growth. The first task is to continue services-led growth at scale by broadening modern services including logistics platforms, tourism, healthcare delivery, education technology, engineering and design and financial services. And the second is to make manufacturing sector more competitive and productivity intensive.

5.1 Free and open market economy

5.1.1 The crisis in 1991 released shackle of License Raj

On August 15, 1947, India gained independence from British colonial rule. Under the leadership of its first Prime Minister, *Jawaharlal Nehru*, the newly independent nation adopted 'democratic socialism' as the guiding principle for both political and economic policies. Nehruvian socialism was rooted in India's struggle for independence and reflected a deep desire to reject foreign domination while promoting national self-reliance. Rather than following the Soviet model of socialism, India created its own system, combining democratic institutions with strong state control over the economy.

The post-independence government pursued a strategy of inward-looking and self-sufficient economic development. The government exercised extensive control over virtually all major economic activities, and public-sector enterprises dominated key industries, including energy, steel, transport, telecommunications and even consumer goods. Economic activities such as investment, trade and factory expansion required government licenses, which was known as the 'License *Raj*'. The government decided on the scale, location and even technology of new industrial projects. Large enterprises were deliberately restrained to leave room for small and technologically backward firms. Financial activities such as opening bank accounts or transferring large sums of money were also subject to licensing.

Economist Jeffrey Sachs characterized this system by observing that "the economy was tied up in horrendous knots so tight that it could hardly grow". Although India achieved political independence, a highly rigid bureaucratic structure emerged that in many ways replaced colonial rule with another form of administrative control. Extensive regulation and state intervention contributed to sluggish economic performance. India's GDP expanded at an average annual rate of about 3.5%, a pace widely described as the "Hindu rate of growth". In 1950–1970, per capita income increased by only 1.9% per year. Although this represented an improvement over the pre-independence period from 1870 to 1947, when per capita growth averaged just 0.2% annually, it remained significantly below the performance of many other Asian economies.

Despite several attempts at reform, the regulatory framework remained largely intact until 1991. Throughout the 1980s, India ran persistent current account deficits, financed primarily by external borrowing. The situation deteriorated in 1990 when Iraq's invasion of Kuwait caused crude oil prices to double from $17 to $34 per barrel. Thousands of Indian workers in Kuwait lost their jobs, cutting off vital remittances. As external debt ballooned, foreign exchange reserves dwindled to barely one month's worth of imports. By mid-1991, India's credit rating was downgraded, blocking access to international credit markets. The government was forced to seek emergency assistance from the IMF and the World Bank, which came with drastic reforms as a precondition of help.

This foreign exchange crisis marked a turning point in India's economic history. In July 1991, Prime Minister *P. V. Narasimha Rao* and Finance Minister *Manmohan Singh* launched a comprehensive economic reform program aimed at liberalizing the economy and embracing market principles. The 1991 reform represented a decisive break from the License *Raj*, shifting the central role in growth from the state to private enterprise. Industrial deregulation, trade liberalization and the promotion of FDI became the key pillars of reform.

Industrial licensing was drastically curtailed. The government replaced the positive list of licensed industries with a negative list, which meant that all industries were open to private investment except those explicitly restricted. Public-sector monopolies were dismantled in sectors such as steel, heavy machinery, telecommunications, oil, mining and air transport. Only three strategic sectors such as defense, atomic energy and railways remained under state control. Import licensing was reduced, and automatic approval of FDI was introduced for up to 51% foreign ownership. Tariffs on non-agricultural goods were progressively lowered to encourage competition and exports.

However, India maintained its long-standing policy of protecting small-scale industries. The Monopolies and Restrictive Trade Practices Act barred large firms from entering sectors reserved for small enterprises. Since the late 1970s, nearly 800 products, including garments, shoes and toys, were reserved for small-scale production with a maximum investment ceiling of $250,000. This policy prevented modernization and large-scale investment, limiting competitiveness in export-oriented industries. Although intended to protect small businesses, it ultimately hindered industrial growth.

Recognizing these limitations, the Report of the Committee on Small Scale Enterprises (1997) and the Report of the Prime Minister's Economic Advisory Council (2001) recommended phasing out the reservation policy. In response, 14 items were de-reserved in 2001 and another 50 in 2002, including key export products such as textiles, toys and auto components. The investment ceiling was also raised to $1 million for certain industries.

While the 1991 crisis undoubtedly marked the beginning of India's liberalization era, the pace of reform was cautious and gradual. Compared with the rapid, externally driven transformations in Japan, Korea and China, India's response to its crisis was far more gradual and cautious. Although this gradualism ensured political stability, it also slowed the country's transition to a high-growth economy, leaving much of its vast economic potential unrealized in the early decades of reform.

5.1.2 Overcoming historical legacies

Since gaining independence in 1947, India had pursued a highly protectionist policy of import-substitution industrialization (ISI). This choice of ISI was not unusual at the time, as the World Bank itself recommended ISI policies to developing countries during the 1950s. The logic behind the policy was straightforward. By restricting imports of consumer goods, the government could protect domestic industries from foreign competition and nurture local production. Import controls consisted of high tariffs, quantitative restrictions and complex licensing procedures, all of which were intended to conserve foreign exchange and promote the development of a self-reliant industrial base.

India's reluctance to open its domestic markets was deeply rooted in history. The country had endured nearly two centuries of foreign domination under the British East India Company and later the British Crown. The painful memory of losing sovereignty to a private trading company left a lasting scar on India's political and economic psyche. As a result, both policymakers and the public developed a strong aversion to foreign trade and investment. Many feared that liberalizing imports would flood the domestic market with cheap foreign goods, undermining local industries and eroding hard-won economic independence.

While the intention behind ISI was to promote domestic industry, in practice, the system bred inefficiency, stagnation and lack of competitiveness. Protected industries had little incentive to innovate or improve productivity. By the 1980s, it became evident that India's inward-looking approach reached its limits. The 1991 balance-of-payments crisis provided political momentum for reform, marking the beginning of a gradual shift toward trade liberalization and economic openness.

The first major step in the reform process was to dismantle the restrictive import regime. Import licensing was phased out gradually. For capital goods and intermediate inputs, the system was abolished in 1993. However, consumer goods imports remained restricted for a longer period due to political resistance from small-scale industries that depended on protection. Quantitative restrictions on imports of consumer goods and agricultural products were finally lifted on April 1, 2001.

Following the reforms, tariff reductions became a central element of trade liberalization. The government systematically reduced both average and peak tariff rates to align with global standards and encourage trade efficiency. The average import duty fell sharply from 72.5% in 1991 to 24.6% in 1996.[1] These reductions reflected a decisive move toward a rules-based trade regime consistent with World Trade Organization (WTO) principles, which India adopted after joining the WTO in 1995.

The reforms dramatically increased India's trade openness. The ratio of exports and imports to GDP rose steadily, indicating the growing importance of international trade in the national economy. Exports as a share of GDP, which averaged only about 6% in the 1980s, climbed to around 22% by the 2010s. The composition of trade also evolved. While traditional exports such as textiles, tea and agricultural goods remained important, new sectors like information technology (IT) services, pharmaceuticals, engineering goods and automobiles emerged as major foreign exchange earners. On the import side, demand shifted toward capital goods, machinery and high-technology components, reflecting industrial modernization.

FDI also became a cornerstone of India's reform agenda. For a developing country like India, FDI was vital not only as a source of capital but also as a conduit for advanced technology, managerial skills and global market access. The inflow of foreign investment helped introduce competition, modernize domestic industries and expand export capacity. Furthermore, FDI alleviated chronic shortages of savings and foreign exchange that had constrained India's development for decades.

To attract foreign investment, the Indian government progressively relaxed restrictions on foreign ownership and participation. Foreign investors were allowed to hold majority ownership up to 100% in most sectors, with a few exceptions such as banking, insurance, telecommunications and airlines. The approval process was also streamlined. The government introduced an automatic approval route, under which foreign equity participation was permitted up to specified limits of 100%, 74% or 51%, depending on the industry. Companies eligible under this route could obtain approval simply by registering with the Reserve Bank of India. Investments outside these limits, or in non-listed sectors, required clearance from the Foreign Investment Promotion Board (FIPB).

In addition, India opened its stock markets to foreign institutional investors in 1993, allowing portfolio investment in listed Indian companies. This reform helped integrate India's financial markets into the global economy, bringing in both capital and investor confidence. Through these combined reforms, trade liberalization, tariff reduction and FDI facilitation, India gradually shifted from a protectionist, inward-looking economy to one increasingly engaged with global markets. Although the process was cautious and incremental, it laid the foundation for India's later emergence as one of the world's fastest-growing economies.

5.2 Accountable government and effective policies

5.2.1 Why economic planning failed in India?

It is often believed, though incorrectly, that India's slow economic progress was mainly due to the absence of coherent economic planning or weak policy implementation. India had a long tradition of formal economic planning well before independence. The National Planning Committee was established by the Indian National Congress in 1938, and in 1944, leading industrialists proposed 'A Plan of Economic Development for India' (widely known as the Bombay Plan). After independence, India officially launched its First Five-Year Plan in 1951, and 12 consecutive plans were implemented until 2017.

Despite having introduced economic planning nearly a decade earlier than Korea, India was soon overtaken by Korea in terms of industrialization and economic growth during the 1960s and 1970s. The key difference was not in the existence of plans but in governance and policy effectiveness. India maintained a democratic system with regular free elections, and thus, its governments were formally accountable to the electorate. However, political accountability did not always translate into economic efficiency.

After independence, capitalism was widely associated with colonial exploitation, and there was strong public sentiment against profit-oriented private enterprise. The prevailing belief was that the state should control production and allocate resources according to social priorities. Influenced by the perceived success of Soviet-style planning, the Indian government adopted a model that placed the state at the 'commanding heights' of the economy.[2] This led to the emergence of an elaborate system of licenses, permits and regulations, collectively known as the 'License *Raj*'. Under this framework, nearly every major economic activity, from establishing a factory to expanding production, required prior government approval.

India's 12 Five-Year Plans (1951–2017) produced a mixed record of achievements and shortcomings. On the positive side, India's economic planning was instrumental in establishing the foundations of a modern economy and promoting social welfare. The Five-Year Plans helped build a broad-based industrial structure; expanded key sectors such as steel, power and transport; and encouraged the growth of education, health care and infrastructure. The Green Revolution of the late 1960s and 1970s was a great success, which transformed India from a food-deficient country to a net agricultural producer. The planning process also promoted social development and expanded employment opportunities.

However, it ultimately fell short in ensuring efficiency, equity and dynamism. The planning model also revealed significant weaknesses. Persistent poverty, unemployment and income inequality remained major challenges despite decades of intervention. Bureaucratic inefficiency, excessive regulation and the dominance of the public sector often led to slow decision-making, waste of resources and poor implementation. The emphasis on import substitution and state control resulted in low productivity, technological stagnation and limited global competitiveness. Fiscal deficits and macroeconomic imbalances grew over time, culminating in the 1991 balance-of-payments crisis, which exposed the structural flaws of the earlier planning system. The lessons of this experience paved the way for the liberalization and market-oriented reforms of the 1990s.

Unlike its East Asian counterparts, India's economic planning placed equality before growth. Political leaders sought to ensure social justice through redistribution and regulation, but this came at the cost of efficiency and competitiveness. Moreover, India's political structure, characterized by linguistic, cultural, ethnic and religious diversity, made it difficult to sustain consensus for long-term developmental goals. In a country of such heterogeneity, democratic governments often resorted to populist policies to secure electoral support. While this made them accountable in a democratic sense, it also constrained them from pursuing difficult but necessary economic reforms.

Significant and persistent obstacles hindered the implementation of reforms through the planning framework. The process of dismantling the extensive system of regulations and controls was slow and politically contentious. Entrenched institutions and vested interests proved far more difficult to reform than to establish. Groups that had benefited from the existing system resisted change, and meaningful reform often occurred only under the pressure of severe crises. Even more than a decade after the 1991 reforms, India continued to face difficulties in unifying its fragmented tax structure, ultimately introducing the Goods and Services Tax (GST) in 2017 to replace a complex network of state-level taxes.

Another major obstacle for implementing the Plans was chronic fiscal deficit. Excessive public spending, often driven by populist measures, absorbed much of the country's domestic savings and crowded out private investment. Fiscal imbalances left the government with little room for essential public investment in infrastructure, education and health. High government borrowing also led to inflationary pressures and limited financial resources for the private sector.

The root cause of this persistent fiscal weakness was India's adherence to the principles of democratic socialism. Both central and state governments intervened heavily in the economy, providing extensive subsidies and welfare programs regardless of their fiscal sustainability. Populist policies, especially around election periods, further widened the deficits. As a result, India's developmental system was large in scope but weak in execution, prioritizing short-term political popularity over long-term economic efficiency.

India's slow progress was not due to a lack of planning but due to the nature of its political economy. While East Asian countries pursued technocratic, performance-based governance focused on growth and competitiveness, India's democratic and populist system prioritized redistribution and political inclusion. This difference in governance, rather than ideology alone, largely explains why India lagged its Asian peers during the decades of high growth in East Asia.

5.2.2 Market decided a different path

India pursued an industrialization path markedly different from that of its East Asian neighbors. While its Asian peers initially focused on labor-intensive manufacturing industries such as textiles, footwear and toys, India's economic growth became increasingly driven by its service sector, particularly IT and software services. Although manufacturing made some progress, it never became the central pillar of industrialization. Instead, services emerged as the major source of exports, employment and foreign exchange, performing the same transformative role that manufacturing had played in East Asia decades earlier.

Following the economic reforms of the early 1990s, India initially saw a modest rise in the share of industry within GDP, but this momentum soon stagnated. In contrast, the share of services expanded rapidly from 30% of GDP in 1950 to 57% in 2008. It became the dominant sector of the economy. Before the reforms, India's service sector had been underdeveloped, largely due to Nehru's emphasis on heavy industry and state-led industrialization. By the 1990s, however, the sector began to grow above the global average, led by new industries such as IT, software development and business process outsourcing.

The rapid rise of the IT service sector in India was primarily driven by market dynamics rather than state direction. Multinational corporations began relocating their back-office operations to India on account of its large pool of English-speaking and technically skilled workers as well as significantly lower labor costs. The trend began in the late 1980s when American Express transferred its back-office operations to India, followed by General Electric in the 1990s. These moves paved the way for India to become the global hub for IT-enabled services.

Unlike manufacturing, the growth of IT and service industries was not constrained by India's weak physical infrastructure. Poor road infrastructure, congested ports and inefficient logistics had long posed significant obstacles to industrial expansion and trade. However, service industries, particularly those based on digital communication, were far less dependent on physical infrastructure. With the expansion of satellite communication and internet connectivity, even firms with limited physical infrastructure could serve clients around the world. Consequently, India became a leading center for software engineering, data processing, computer graphics, customer support and other IT-enabled business services.

Another reason for this shift was the technological context of the 1990s. When Japan, Korea and other Asian economies industrialized during 1950s–1980s, IT had not yet revolutionized global production. India, as a latecomer, was integrated into the global economy when IT was becoming central to business operations. This timing allowed India to leapfrog traditional industrialization and specialize in software development, IT consulting and related services. New business niches such as medical transcription, accounting outsourcing and customer service flourished. Exports of IT and software services surged from just $100 million in 1990 to $6 billion in 2000, growing at an annual rate of 20%.

Private companies, both domestic and foreign, were the main drivers of this transformation. Texas Instruments was among the first to establish a 100% export-oriented software subsidiary in India. Tata Consultancy Services (TCS), founded in 1974, marked the beginning of India's software export industry. During the 1970s and 1980s, the government sought to promote both the hardware and software sectors, but high import tariffs and regulatory complexity hampered progress. Recognizing these constraints, the government revised its computer policy in 1984 and began actively encouraging software exports and foreign investment.

A key institutional development was the establishment of the Software Technology Parks of India (STPI) in 1990. These parks which were set up in Bangalore, Pune and Bhubaneshwar offered advanced infrastructure, full foreign equity ownership and tax incentives to export-oriented firms. By 2005, over 5,800 firms were registered under the STPI scheme, accounting for 95% of India's software exports. Further liberalization followed with the 1986 Software Policy, which simplified regulations, provided tax exemptions for software exports and allowed duty-free imports of hardware for export production.

The 1991 liberalization program under Prime Minister *P.V. Narasimha Rao* and Finance Minister *Manmohan Singh* further improved the business environment. Barriers to foreign investment were dismantled, restrictions on technology transfers were relaxed and private participation in policymaking was encouraged. The government also facilitated venture capital financing for IT startups and undertook major telecommunication reforms, reducing costs and expanding access to digital networks.

Despite the sector's success, some economists have questioned whether India's IT-led growth model can deliver broad-based growth of economy. They argue that the service sector, particularly IT and software, relies on highly skilled labor and does not generate sufficient employment for the vast numbers of low- and semi-skilled workers who still dominate India's labor force. Unlike East Asia's manufacturing-led growth, which absorbed millions of workers from agriculture, India's service sector expansion has created a 'jobless growth' dilemma. India's path shows a unique model of development which has been driven not by factories and exports of goods but by code, data and digital services. The answer is still open and depends on the country's ability to capitalize on global technological change and its human capital and to advance the linkage between serve and manufacture sector.

5.3 Education and human resource development

5.3.1 Deep but narrow education

Baumol categorized national education systems as either 'deep' or 'wide'.[3] According to his framework, India's education system was 'deep', while countries such as Japan, Korea and China adopted 'wide' education systems during their periods of rapid economic development. In other words, India's education policy concentrated on nurturing a small number of elites rather than providing broad-based education for the entire population.

India inherited a colonial education structure that emphasized higher education, particularly universities, because the British administration needed middle-level managers and civil servants. After independence, the Indian government continued this orientation in the 1950s, focusing on elite technical education. It established two world-class institutions, the Indian Institutes of Technology (IIT) in 1958 and the Indian Institutes of Management (IIM) in 1961, to cultivate top-tier engineers, scientists and administrators.

For nearly four decades after independence, India's education policy remained heavily biased toward tertiary technical education, with limited attention to elementary and vocational schooling. This neglect of basic education from the 1950s to the 1990s resulted in millions of workers entering the labor force without completing primary education. Many critics argued that heavy investment in universities came at the expense of literacy and basic education, widening inequality in human capital formation. Although India's Constitution explicitly recognized education as a fundamental right, implementation lagged political rhetoric. The government gradually expanded free and compulsory primary education, but progress was slow. In 1954, only 7% of India's population attended school, compared to 17% in Korea and 23% in Japan.

It took until the 1990s for India to see significant progress in basic education. The national literacy rate rose more rapidly than before, reaching 65% in 2001, with notable gains in less developed states such as *Bihar*, *Madhya Pradesh*, *Uttar Pradesh* and *Rajasthan*. The proportion of people aged 15 and older with no schooling dropped from 66.2% in 1970 to 51.6% in 1990 and further to 32.7% in 2010. Average years of total schooling increased from 1.6 years in 1970 to 5.1 years in 2010. Among younger cohorts aged 15–24, the improvement was even greater. No schooling declined from 52.3% in 1970 to just 7.1% in 2010, and average years of schooling rose from 2.5 to 7.1 years over the same period.

Enrollment rates for primary education rose impressively from 57% in 1970 to universal coverage by 2005. However, progress in secondary education was slower, with enrollment rates increasing from 20% in 1970 to 51.3% in 2005, while tertiary education rates grew from 8.2% to 9.1% in the same period.

India's focus on a deep education system led to the neglect of basic education. As a result, it widened social and economic inequality and incurred the mismatch between education and employment for decades. And this limited productivity growth in agriculture and manufacturing. However, there was a bright side of the India's deep education system. This system emphasized excellence in higher education and prioritized science and engineering over social sciences and the arts. It also provided the intellectual foundation for India's modernization and integration into the global economy. The presence of well-trained engineers, scientists and policymakers allowed India to absorb and adapt advanced technologies and to participate in high-value sectors such as software development, pharmaceuticals and space technology. It also supported domestic capacity for research, planning and industrial development.

This focus on advanced technical education significantly contributed to India's later success in the service and IT sectors. Investments in higher education, particularly in the IITs, produced a pool of highly skilled engineers and computer scientists who became the backbone of India's software and IT-enabled services industries. The educated elite at IIT and IIM contributed significantly to India's technological progress and later became instrumental in the rise of the information technology and service industries from the 1990s onward.

To further strengthen this advantage, the government upgraded the Department of Electronics into the Ministry of Information Technology in 2000 and encouraged private investment in IT education. These policies expanded the supply of skilled professionals and helped position India as a global hub for information technology, software development and digital services.

5.3.2 Bengaluru, hub of IT and software industry

Bengaluru has emerged as the center of India's IT and software industry. Major Indian technology firms such as TCS, Infosys, and Wipro were founded in Bengaluru, and numerous IT ventures have clustered in the city over the decades. The main reason for Bengaluru's rise as India's 'Silicon Valley' lies in its strong foundation of higher education and research institutions.

Among these, the Indian Institute of Science (IISc) stands at the core of Bengaluru's academic ecosystem. Established in 1909, IISc became India's premier institution for advanced scientific research and technological education. The institute attracts the best graduates from the Indian Institutes of Technology (IITs), which are in seven major cities across the country. The Indian Institute of Management (IIM) in Bengaluru, modeled after Harvard Business School, further strengthens the city's academic and professional environment.

Bengaluru was also home to three major military state enterprises which are Hindustan Aeronautics Limited (HAL), Bharat Earth Movers Limited (BEML), and Bharat Electronics Limited (BEL). These defense-related industries established the city's early reputation as a center for advanced technology, aerospace, and electronics. Building on this foundation, the Indian government established the Software Technology Park (STP) in Bengaluru in 1991 to promote IT exports. Companies in the STP received a range of incentives, including tax benefits, simplified customs clearance, and streamlined incorporation procedures. This policy attracted global technology giants such as Microsoft, IBM, HP, Motorola, AT&T, and Samsung to set up offices in Bengaluru.

The city's success also stemmed from its vast pool of skilled and cost-effective labor. Every year, Indian universities and technical institutes produced more than 100,000 IT professionals, many of whom were fluent in English, well-trained, and highly motivated. The combination of affordable talent, favorable policies, and a vibrant ecosystem made Bengaluru an attractive destination for both domestic and international companies.

Private institutions played an essential role in supporting the rise of the city. By the 2000s, about 85% of undergraduate engineering education in India was provided by privately managed colleges. Leading IT firms and industry associations, including TCS and NASSCOM, often raised concerns about the mismatch between graduates' skills and market demands. To address this issue, major IT companies such as TCS, Infosys and Wipro established their own training centers and partnered with universities to design curricula aligned with industry needs. As a result, the average corporate training duration at TCS, for example, decreased from 76 to 52 days, reflecting improved graduate readiness for employment.

India's human capital development was also shaped by its global diaspora. While many Asian countries benefited from foreign-educated professionals, India's experience was remarkable in both scale and impact. From the 1970s to the 1990s, millions of Indian professionals migrated abroad, initially due to limited domestic job opportunities. Over time, migration patterns shifted from low-skilled labor to highly skilled professionals in the fields of technology, medicine and engineering. By the late 1990s, Indian engineers, together with Chinese, were estimated to be leading nearly 30% of technology businesses in Silicon Valley.

This phenomenon, once seen as a 'brain drain', evolved into what scholars now call 'brain circulation'. As India's economy expanded and its IT sector flourished, many skilled Indian professionals returned home, bringing with them global expertise, managerial experience and valuable networks. Their return strengthened domestic industries, inspired entrepreneurship and accelerated technological innovation.[4] By 2015, the number of Indian emigrants had reached 10.4 million, up from 3.7 million in 2005. Although emigration continued, the flow of returnees and their contributions to India's economy transformed the earlier loss of talent into a source of renewed growth and competitiveness for the nation's high-tech industries.

5.4 Savings and investment, leading to capital accumulation

5.4.1 Unfinished mission, land reform and green revolution

In India, landlessness was one of the main determinants of poverty. Small and fragmented landholdings constrained agricultural productivity, while deep-rooted power asymmetries enabled landlords to extract tenants' surpluses through high and often arbitrary rents. These exploitative arrangements eroded tenants' incentives to invest and made it nearly impossible for poor cultivators to accumulate either human or physical capital. Land reform was therefore considered essential not only to reduce poverty but also to raise agricultural output by increasing tenure security and redistributing land to cultivators.

The Indian government continued to pursue land reform and improve land administration after independence. The first wave of reforms in the 1950s sought to abolish the long-standing '*zamindari* system' (meaning permanent settlement), which had been introduced by the British at the end of the 18th century. Under this system, feudal landlords were declared landowners, while peasants became tenants who paid rents which were collected through a chain of intermediaries. Although zamindari was legally abolished, implementation varied widely across states due to differences in local political will and administrative capacity.[5]

The second wave of reform, through the 1950s and 1960s, aimed to regulate tenancy by capping rents and granting ownership rights to actual cultivators. New tenancy laws strengthened tenure security, restricted rent levels and required registration of tenancy agreements. These measures reduced the risk of eviction and allowed tenants to retain a greater share of their harvests. However, in some areas, these regulations pushed tenancy arrangements underground, making it harder to identify and formalize the rights of sharecroppers.

The third wave, from the 1960s into the 1970s, sought to impose ceilings on landholdings and redistribute surplus land to landless or marginal farmers. Ceiling laws empowered the state to expropriate land above prescribed limits and reallocate it to poorer households. Despite widespread evasion and loopholes, these policies achieved significant outcomes. By the 1980s, around 5.7 million households received an average of 0.4 hectares each through redistribution. In total, ownership rights over approximately ten million hectares were transferred to tenant farmers. This area was greater than the combined redistributed lands of Japan, Korea and Taiwan following their own reforms. Yet, the national impact remained uneven, as the most successful reforms were concentrated in a few progressive states.

The transfer of land from large estates to small owner-cultivators increased productivity by creating direct incentives for hard work and efficient management. Nonetheless, the broader goals of equity and nationwide productivity growth were not fully realized. Weak enforcement, political resistance from powerful landowners, fragmented state systems and poor land records hindered the full potential of reform.

By the late 1960s, policy attention shifted toward technological change in agriculture through the Green Revolution. India invested heavily in irrigation, improved seed varieties, fertilizers and pesticides.[6] The adoption of high-yield varieties of wheat and rice, particularly in Punjab and Haryana, transformed these regions into the most productive and prosperous in the country. The Green Revolution enabled India to overcome chronic food shortages and achieve self-sufficiency in grain production by the 1980s,[7] an era during which the population had nearly doubled.

The early land reforms played a foundational role in enabling the Green Revolution. By weakening the feudal structure and enhancing rural social stability, these reforms made sustained public investment in infrastructure possible. Investments in irrigation, drainage, soil conservation, water management, rural roads, electrification and education dramatically improved the agricultural environment. Subsidies for fertilizer, water and electricity further boosted productivity. Over time, secure land rights and rising rural incomes facilitated farm mechanization and allowed surplus labor to move into non-farm employment, increasing overall economic productivity.

Ultimately, the effects of India's land reforms and the Green Revolution were nuanced and varied across states. Land reform contributed to growth where it successfully strengthened cultivators' property rights, allowed flexible and legal land leasing and was complemented by investments in irrigation, credit and infrastructure.[8] Land reform and the Green Revolution together reshaped India's agrarian structure, laying the groundwork for rural transformation and long-term economic development.

5.4.2 Affinity for gold

Low incomes and weak domestic savings trapped the Indian economy in a persistent cycle of underinvestment and slow growth. In the late 1980s, Prime Minister *Rajiv Gandhi* introduced limited market-oriented reforms aimed at revitalizing the economy, but these efforts proved short-lived and largely ineffective. One of the main reasons for the failure was India's heavy dependence on foreign borrowing to finance investment projects. The accumulation of external debt eroded investor confidence, leading to rapid capital outflows and ultimately a balance-of-payments crisis. To achieve sustainable growth, it became essential for India to mobilize sufficient domestic savings to fund productive investment.

The comparison with Korea clearly reveals India's relative weakness in mobilizing domestic savings. Between 1961 and 1964, India's savings rate averaged 14.3%, while Korea's was only 4.4%. However, Korea's savings rate rose sharply to 13% during 1965–1969 and to 35.9% by 1990–1998. In contrast, India's rate increased only modestly from 15.0% in 1965–1969 to 24.2% during 1990–1998. This widening gap illustrates India's limited capacity to mobilize domestic savings, which in turn constrained its ability to finance higher levels of investment and sustain faster economic growth.

A challenge for India's economy was that most household wealth was tied up in non-financial assets such as gold, precious gems and lands. This strong cultural and economic preference for gold limited the amount of money flowing into the formal financial system. According to the World Gold

Council, Indian households together hold around 25,000 tons of gold, worth trillions of dollars, making India one of the largest private holders of gold in the world.

To address this issue, the government introduced the Gold Control Act of 1968, which banned private ownership of gold bars and coins and restricted gold imports. However, instead of reducing demand, the law encouraged large-scale gold smuggling. Although the policy was intended to shift household wealth from unproductive assets toward financial investments, it ultimately had limited success in achieving that goal.

The preference for gold, however, cannot be explained solely as a matter of cultural tradition. It also reflected structural weaknesses in India's financial and macroeconomic systems. Episodes of high and volatile inflation, negative real interest rates on deposits and financial repression made formal savings unattractive. In such an environment, gold served both as a hedge against inflation and as a secure, liquid store of value. Moreover, golden jewelry's dual role as adornment and as a precautionary asset further reinforced its prominence in household wealth.

Since independence, the Indian government has consistently worked to increase domestic savings. In the early years, the main goal was to create safe and accessible financial channels for ordinary citizens. This effort, often referred to as 'social banking', focused on mobilizing household deposits through a growing network of public savings institutions. The government promoted small savings schemes, especially those operated through the postal system, which became a trusted savings avenue for millions. Instruments such as the National Savings Certificates (NSCs) and Post Office Savings Accounts formed the core of early domestic savings mobilization.

Between 1969 and 1991, after the nationalization of banks,[9] the introduction of the Lead Bank Scheme[10] further strengthened this effort by driving a large expansion of bank branches into rural and semi-urban areas. This not only improved access to financial services but also played a key role in enhancing financial inclusion across the country.

After the 1991 economic reforms, the liberalization of interest rates and the opening of capital markets diversified saving channels beyond traditional bank deposits. Mutual funds began to grow rapidly, followed by the expansion of private insurance and pension markets. These changes gradually deepened India's financial system and increased the formal savings rate, but important structural gaps persisted.

India gradually improved its domestic savings performance. Household savings rose from about 17% of GDP in the 1990s to 23% in the 2010s. The Post Office Savings Bank (POSB) expanded to more than 154,000 branches by the late 1990s, reaching deep into rural areas. Even so, total household financial savings amounted to only about 11% of GDP, significantly lower than in high-performing East Asian economies.

Notes

1 Likewise, the basic customs duty rate was reduced from 22% in 1991 to 4% in 2002, while the peak tariff rate dropped from an extremely high 150% to 30.8% during the same period.

2 Made in India, Amitabh Kant, p21.

3 A 'deep' education system focuses on producing a limited number of highly educated elites—scientists, engineers, administrators and intellectuals—while a 'wide' education system aims to provide broad-based education across the entire population, emphasizing literacy, numeracy and basic vocational skills.

4 Naoyuki Yoshino, et al., Determinants of International Remittance Inflows in Middle-Income Countries in Asia and Pacific, 2019, ADBI Working Paper, p15.

5 Many large landlords retained control through litigation or by reorganizing holdings within families and trusts.

6 Green Revolution strengthened medium and large farmers who could secure irrigation and credit, while marginal and tenant farmers in rainfed areas saw fewer benefits.

7 In 2016, India became the world's largest rice exporter, surpassing Thailand, Bangladesh, the People's Republic of China and Vietnam.

8 In areas where land redistribution was incomplete, records were weak or tenancy was driven underground, reforms had limited—and sometimes even negative—economic effects.

9 Before 1969, India's banking system was largely in private hands and concentrated in urban centers. This led to serious credit imbalances and financial exclusion in large parts of the country.

In July 1969, the government nationalized 14 major commercial banks, followed by the nationalization of six more in 1980. The goal was to bring banking under public ownership so that it could serve social and developmental objectives, especially channeling credit to priority sectors such as agriculture, small industries and rural development.

10 The Lead Bank Scheme of 1969 was a landmark initiative in India's banking history that helped extend the reach of institutional credit to rural and semi-urban areas. By designating a lead bank for each district, the scheme created an organized framework for district-level credit planning and coordination. Although its effectiveness has declined in recent decades, the scheme laid the foundation for inclusive banking and remains an integral part of India's efforts to ensure equitable regional development and financial inclusion.

6 Asia's Ongoing Journey to Prosperity

6.1 Lessons from the journey up to here

Sustained economic growth cannot be achieved by following a simple or universal formula. A successful development strategy requires the right combination of elements, applied with appropriate timing and effective implementation. Economic growth is not like a modern food delivery service. There is no ready-made solution that arrives at the doorstep. Each country must instead enter the marketplace of ideas, select its ingredients with care and craft its own recipe for success.

Some nations may find that their resources and conditions are best suited for growing rice, while others may be better positioned to produce wheat. Some may possess the institutions and tools to advance rapidly, while others must first build the foundations necessary for development. The experiences of the Four Asian Geese therefore do not offer a fixed model to replicate but rather a valuable reference for countries seeking their own path toward high growth and lasting prosperity.

6.1.1 Chairs keep balance with four legs

There is a common adage, "Once begun is half done". *Jeffrey Sachs* has observed that growth often appears self-reinforcing as higher capital stocks, deeper specialization, advancing technology and lower fertility move together. Taking at face value, this suggests that economic take-off leads almost automatically to sustained expansion. The historical record of the past century, however, does not support so optimistic a view. Many developing countries have struggled to achieve an initial take-off and even more have found it difficult to maintain momentum. Stagnation and reversals have been frequent. Sustained and uninterrupted growth episodes are the exception rather than the rule.

In this book, I am arguing that sustained growth rests on four mutually reinforcing building blocks: a free and open market economy; an accountable government that implements effective policies; education and human resource development and savings and investment, leading to capital accumulation.

DOI: 10.4324/9781003797135-6

The central claim is straightforward. Without all four building blocks in reasonably balanced form, economies never sustain rapid growth.

Even with less than four legs, a chair has no chance to stand firmly. The chair with only one leg or two can stand only in a few seconds. The chair with three legs can stand by itself but it can neither last longer in shaky situation nor endure the heavier weight. The economy can start an economic take-off without all four pillars but cannot sustain the momentum longer enough to lead to economic prosperity. The economy must try to keep the four legs with the same length for balancing. Although an economy takes a successful take-off and sustains growth for some time, it is likely to collapse if it does not keep a balance because the outcome of the growth may make one leg longer than others.

The four pillars must keep a balance in the whole process of growth. A table cannot bear weight if one leg is much shorter than the others. India's much lag in growth in postwar period illustrates the risks of imbalance. Despite a robust democratic framework and abundant labor, policies did not consistently translate these strengths into investment and productivity gains. When India broadened economic freedom and openness beginning in 1991, it was able to embark on a more durable growth path.

Korea offers an example of how a country worked continuously to maintain balance during its economic growth. During 1960s–1970s, Korea achieved remarkable progress after two decades of rapid industrial expansion. As a result, its economy became more open and market-oriented, supported by a better-educated workforce and a new generation of prudent, forward-looking entrepreneurs, unlike in the 1960s. However, while the economy advanced rapidly, political development lagged, creating a serious imbalance between economic and political institutions. This imbalance was corrected through the democratic movement of the 1980s, which brought significant political reforms. Through this transformation, Korea was able to restore balance among its key pillars of development, achieving both an accountable government and effective policymaking to support sustained growth.

The lesson for latecomer economies is clear: growth does not follow automatically once development begins. Sustained progress requires continuous effort to maintain a balance among well-functioning markets, capable and accountable government, sustained human-capital formation and the effective mobilization of savings and investment.

6.1.2 There is no such thing as one size fits all

Joe Studwell famously wrote, "The recipe for success has been as simple: one is household farming, two is export-oriented manufacturing, and three is closely controlled finance that supports these two sectors". Indeed, with those measures, the Four Asian Geese demonstrated remarkable success in launching and sustaining rapid economic growth. Yet, despite the apparent simplicity of Studwell's formula, many other Asian economies have failed to replicate this success. A closer look at the Four Asian Geese's growth trajectories in the previous chapters reveals that the path to growth is far more complex than Studwell's concise prescription suggests.

Many Asian economies were unable to implement Studwell's 'simple recipe' due to a range of factors, including structural constraints and political instability. For small island nations in the Pacific, for instance, household farming and mass manufacturing are inherently impractical due to limited arable land and low population density. Other countries such as Afghanistan, Myanmar and North Korea have been paralyzed by internal conflict, authoritarian rule and isolation, leaving them unable to implement coherent development strategies. These cases demonstrate that Studwell's formula, while insightful, cannot serve as a universal silver bullet for economic transformation.

Studwell's three-part model can nonetheless be interpreted more broadly as a framework for early-stage economic development. Household farming and light manufacturing represent not merely sectoral choices but fundamental economic mechanisms. They help generate domestic savings, promote productivity growth and instill the discipline and competition essential to a market-based economy. In this context, his concept of 'controlled finance' signifies more than simple state intervention. It refers to accountable public institutions capable of channeling financial resources toward strategic sectors in support of long-term development. Interpreted in this way, Studwell's prescription is broadly consistent with the four pillars employed in this book.

Historically, industrialization through manufacturing has been the most reliable engine of rapid economic growth. In most successful cases, the share of manufacturing in total output and employment expanded dramatically during the development process. For example, manufacturing accounted for around 30% of China's GDP, with industrial employment rising to 22% by 2018. However, India diverged sharply from this pattern. Since the 1970s, India's manufacturing share has remained stagnant, roughly 16% of output and 11% of employment. Instead, its services sector surged from 43% of GDP in 1990 to 57% by 2009.

What explains this divergence? Manufacturing industries traditionally have stronger multiplier effects because economies of scale make mass production highly efficient. India, by contrast, embraced a service-led model as information technology advanced in the 1990s. The digital revolution allowed services such as software, telecommunications and business process outsourcing to be traded internationally, making service-led growth more feasible than ever before. This illustrates that in today's global economy, multiple pathways to industrialization are emerging, depending on technological conditions and comparative advantage.

The role of government in economic development has also varied widely across Asia. The experience of the Four Asian Geese demonstrates that rapid growth often requires a hybrid of state intervention and market mechanisms.

Despite the different degrees and extent of their intervention, they upheld basics of private enterprise, market competition and openness of trade and investment. The traditional dichotomy between 'market versus state' is misleading. Successful development depends not on choosing one over the other but on finding the right balance between market dynamism and effective state guidance. The Four Asian Geese differed in which industries they prioritized, which instruments they used and how intensively and how long they intervened.

6.2 Facing changing weather and height

Like migratory birds adapting to changing winds and climates, Asian economies must continuously adjust their policies and strategies to ever-changing surroundings. Economic development is not a linear process but a dynamic and evolving one that demands constant adaptation. What worked in one era may fail in another. As circumstances change, the policies that once drove success can readily become the very constraints that hinder progress.

Bai Gao, a Chinese-born political economist, noted that the very institutions that propelled Japan's economic miracle in the 1960s and 1970s became sources of stagnation in later decades. In his book, *Japan's Economic Dilemma: The Institutional Origins of Prosperity and Stagnation*, he argues that the same institutional structures such as close government–industry coordination and protected financial systems that fueled Japan's high growth in the 1950s–1970s contributed to slower growth and structural inertia in later decades.

6.2.1 End of catch-up and deceleration

Historically, Asia was once the most prosperous region in the world, home to nearly 60% of the global population. Civilizations in China and India flourished for thousands of years before the rise of the West in the 17th and 18th centuries. However, Asia began to fall behind following the European Renaissance in the 15th century, and the gap widened dramatically after the Industrial Revolution in the late 18th century. Today, Asia is again rising. The key question now is whether Asia can not only catch up with the West but also reclaim its historical position as the world's center of civilization and economic power. If Asian economies maintain the pace of growth achieved over the past three decades, such a future may indeed be within reach.

However, history cautions against simple extrapolations from past performance. Four decades ago, Japan was projected to match the US in total GDP by the year 2000. This prediction failed to materialize. In 2010, Japan's GDP was only 34.1% that of the US, compared with 30.6% in 1973.[1] Similar overly optimistic forecasts have been made for China in recent decades, based on projected growth rates of 8%–10%. Many analysts once believed China would surpass the US by 2020, which proved wrong. China's ascent to the top of the global economy has been slower than anticipated.

As examined throughout this book, the contributions of a 'free and open market economy' and 'accountable government' with 'effective policies' diminish once developing economies narrow their gap with advanced economies. For the Four Asian Geese, institutional reforms played a decisive role in achieving rapid growth. The establishment of modern political and economic systems provided the foundation for transformation and served as a 'big push' that reduced institutional barriers, lowered transaction costs and inspired people to work productively and creatively. Such positive impact naturally diminishes as reforms get settled and ordinarily.

Every advanced economy eventually transitions from factor-driven growth, based on labor and capital inputs, to efficiency and innovation-driven growth. Sustainable prosperity in advanced stages depends not merely on numbers of labor and capital accumulation but on creativity, productivity, and entrepreneurship. As *William Baumol* and his colleagues observed, "Entrepreneurial capitalism has powered the USA economy toward a higher growth rate since the 1990s". This model, anchored in innovation and entrepreneurial dynamism, provides a good reference which the Four Asian Geese may to see.

Access to technology, a key driver of development, is also undergoing fundamental change. During their early industrialization, the Four Asian Geese could import advanced technologies through foreign licensing, machinery imports, technical cooperation and foreign direct investment (FDI). Today, they must develop, deploy and innovate technologies on their own. These demands coordinated effort among universities, firms and governments. To meet this challenge, Asian governments are increasingly investing in human capital and innovation systems including training engineers and scientists, supporting research institutions and national laboratories and establishing science and technology parks.

Today, the challenge for the Four Asian Geese is that there is no longer a ready-made development model to follow. The experience and knowledge of their Western predecessors no longer apply seamlessly to their circumstances. They must now chart their own paths, at their own cost, through an era of technological disruption, demographic shifts and global uncertainty. Moreover, the more democratic and pluralistic their societies become, the more complex and contested policy implementation becomes. Future progress will require experimentation, flexibility and tolerance for failure, which inevitably becomes an iterative process of 'trial and error' at higher economic and social costs.

6.2.2 Fragmented global economy

Over the past four decades, the global environment has been broadly favorable to the Four Asian Geese, allowing them to sustain high rates of economic growth. These economies benefited from open access to international markets and from abundant global financing that supported rapid industrialization and investment. Before the collapse of the Soviet Union in 1991, the world economy was divided into two blocs. Within the US-led capitalist bloc, Japan and South Korea leveraged access to vast export markets, benefited from technology transfer and attracted FDI. They were also supported by preferential trade arrangements that promoted their export-led growth. Multilateral trade negotiations, most notably the Kennedy and Uruguay Rounds, helped reduce global tariffs and non-tariff barriers.

China and India, however, were largely excluded from this open trading and investment system until the late 20th century. Their deliberate ideological decisions to remain insulated from global markets significantly constrained their early economic growth. When China embarked on market-oriented reforms and opened its doors to trade and foreign investment in 1989, it was able to capitalize on an increasingly liberalized global economy and integrate rapidly into global supply chains. India was slower to follow. Deeply influenced by the legacy of colonial rule, India maintained a cautious stance toward external influence and preferred inward-looking, protectionist policies. This delayed the adoption of liberalization reforms and postponed the gains that come from global economic integration.

In recent years, however, the liberal and rules-based economic order that once facilitated this growth has come under strain. The global trading environment has become less conducive to growth as the US, historically a leading proponent of free trade, shifted away from its open-market stance. The US imposed new tariffs, withdrew from several free trade agreements and expanded export controls on strategic technologies, while other countries have increasingly followed the suit of the US. The result is a more fragmented global economy, in which the flow of goods, capital, technology, data and people is increasingly governed by competing political and regulatory blocs rather than a unified, multilateral system.

Unlike earlier protectionist waves, mainly adopted by developing countries, that aimed to protect infant industries, the new protectionism is driven primarily by concerns over national security, technological sovereignty, supply-chain resilience and industrial and climate policy. The instruments of protection have also evolved. Instead of relying on broad tariffs and quotas, governments now employ sophisticated measures such as export controls on advanced semiconductors and manufacturing equipment, inbound and outbound investment screening, local-content rules, restrictions on cloud and data infrastructure and large targeted subsidies for strategic industries.

China lies at the center of this new global fragmentation, while Japan, Korea and India are also increasingly affected. As the Four Asian Geese became key exporters of advanced technologies and high-value goods, they find themselves direct targets of these restrictive measures. Whereas earlier forms of protectionism constrained exports of labor-intensive goods like textiles and steel, today's restrictions strike at the heart of high-technology production. They limit access to essential inputs and technologies in areas such as semiconductor fabrication equipment, advanced GPUs, battery materials, rare-earth processing, telecommunications infrastructure and artificial intelligence (AI) services.

For developing countries, the consequences of this new protectionist environment are particularly severe. Shrinking export markets, disrupted economies of scale, higher input and capital costs, slower diffusion of technology and reduced foreign investment collectively hinder the classic model of export-led industrialization. Learning-by-exporting which has been a vital mechanism for capability building is disrupted. Trade-policy uncertainty further discourages long-term investment. The erosion of multilateral cooperation weakens the role of global institutions such as World Trade Organization (WTO) and multilateral development banks (MDBs), leaving developing nations with fewer tools and less support to navigate these challenges.

In theory, global fragmentation could spur productivity through intensified competition. In practice, the opposite is expected to occur. Rivalry between major powers increasingly takes the form of political maneuvering and exclusionary strategies rather than efficiency-driven competition. The emphasis shifts from 'competing to innovate' to 'strategically excluding competitors', undermining both innovation and the diffusion of best practices. The costs of this fractured world fall disproportionately on developing economies, which depend most heavily on open markets, stable trade rules and access to global technologies to drive their growth.

6.2.3 From demographic bonus to onus

Over the past half century, Asia achieved faster and more sustained economic growth than any other region in the world. What made possible this remarkable performance? Many scholars, especially Western economists, attributed Asia's success to its demographic dividend. They argued that rapid growth in the working-age population, rising labor participation and mass urban migration supplied an abundant and youthful workforce that fueled industrial expansion. Improved health, hygiene and medical care further reinforced this advantage. In 1994, *Paul Krugman* famously claimed that the Asian Tigers' growth[2] was largely input-driven, based on labor and capital accumulation rather than productivity gains, and therefore could not last.

Krugman's argument was only half correct. While it is true that the initial phase of Asia's rise depended heavily on labor and capital input, later studies have shown that technological progress and productivity growth also played a crucial role. The Four Asian Geese did not simply grow by working harder. They also learned to work smarter. Through innovation, industrial upgrading and technological diffusion, they began to catch up with the West. The next stage of their development now depends on advancing from technology adoption to technology innovation, supported by robust R&D capacity.

The Four Asian Geese undeniably benefited from demographic advantages. The region experienced sharp and sustained declines in infant and child mortality beginning in the 1950s.[3] While the average East Asian woman bore six children in 1950, she has two today. This demographic transition produced a 'window of opportunity' when the working-age population grew faster than dependents, allowing economies to channel resources into investment and growth. Labor-intensive manufacturing such as textiles, apparel and electronics was the first engine of industrialization, providing mass employment and setting the foundation for later technological advancement.[4]

However, this demographic dividend is now fading. Japan has long entered a post-dividend era, Korea ended dividend era and China's advantage is rapidly eroding. Only India continues to enjoy a young and expanding workforce. The pace of aging in East Asia is far faster than that experienced by the US and Europe. By 2040, the median age in Japan and Korea will reach around 53 years, compared with 42 years in the US. China faces an even greater challenge, as it is growing old before it grows rich, confronting rapid population aging at a much lower level of per capita income than Japan and Korea did.

Japan today is the world's most aged society, with the highest life expectancy globally. In 1950, 12 workers supported one pensioner. Today, that ratio has fallen to just two. The postwar baby boom (1947–1949) produced over 2.5 million births annually, but since 2016, births have fallen below 1 million per year. Korea's demographic shift has been even more dramatic. It is now the fastest-aging country in the world, with the lowest fertility rate and its total population began shrinking in 2020. The working-age (15–64) share is projected to fall from 73.1% in 2012 to 49.7% by 2030.

To cope with this transformation, the Four Asian Geese must prepare for an era of aging and slower population growth. Life expectancy in the region has risen from 43 years in 1950 to around 72 years today, while annual population growth has plunged from 2.4% in the late 1960s to a projected 0.2% by 2025. By 2030, half of the world's elderly population will live in Asia, and one in five Asians will be over 60 years old. Governments will need to promote flexible labor markets, expand female labor participation and liberalize immigration to offset declining workforces. Pension systems and healthcare budgets will come under strain as the number of retirees rises and the labor force contracts.

Demographic change affects growth by reducing the contribution of education and human capital development. The education system must therefore evolve. Its primary mission will shift from producing large quantities of labor force to fostering creative and adaptable talent. Education in the region must also become more diversified and creativity-oriented. To thrive in a globalized knowledge economy, Asian universities must cultivate globally minded and innovative thinkers.

Looking forward, the Four Asian Geese must navigate the transition from demographic dividend to digital dividend. As their labor pools shrink, they must rely on AI, robotics, automation and digital technologies to sustain productivity growth. Encouragingly, the region is already at the forefront of this transformation. Japan combines deep expertise in mechatronics, robotics and factory automation. Korea has the world's highest robot density in manufacturing and dominates in advanced semiconductor technologies such as high-bandwidth memory (HBM). China is competing head-to-head with the US in AI platforms and chip design. India, meanwhile, boasts advanced digital infrastructure and a vast, English-speaking developer base that can accelerate AI adoption.

Demography may no longer be Asia's engine, and technology can become its new driver. By embracing innovation, digitalization and AI-powered productivity, the Four Asian Geese can sustain their long-run ascent, turning the challenge of aging into an opportunity for smarter, more inclusive and more resilient growth.

6.3 Way forward in the future

Many forecasts paint an optimistic picture of Asia's future. The Asian Development Bank (ADB), for instance, projects that Asia's share of global output would rise from 28% in 2010 to over 50% by 2050, and per capita income would increase sixfold during the same period.[5] However, such a bright future is far from guaranteed. Economic growth is a long and rough journey marked by recurring and unexpected challenges, and the success of the past does not ensure success in the future. The Four Asian Geese need to prioritize the quality of growth over its quantity, integrate environmental stewardship and enhance equality among people and countries. In doing so, they can chart a new model of growth, ensuring that Asia's next rise is not only faster but also cleaner and more enduring.

6.3.1 Sustainable development

Over the past several decades, the major Asian economies have experienced remarkable economic expansion, with average annual growth rates of about 8%–10% in Japan, Korea and China and 6%–7% in India. This rapid growth enabled substantial income convergence with advanced economies, consistent with the standard convergence hypothesis. When the technological gap between developing economies and the global frontier is wide, latecomers can grow rapidly by adopting and adapting existing technologies. As this gap narrows, however, sustaining such high growth becomes increasingly difficult, and a gradual slowdown in growth is both expected and economically natural.

Empirical studies show that economic growth tends to slow noticeably once countries reach per capita income levels of roughly $13,000, a threshold already crossed by Japan and Korea and one that China and India are now approaching. Japan's experience is illustrative. Its spectacular growth during the 1950s and 1960s gave way to more moderate expansion in the

1970s and 1980s. Following the asset price collapse in 1991, Japan entered a prolonged period of stagnation, with average growth of about 1% over the next three decades. Korea followed a similar path, rapid industrialization in the 1960s–1980s, a sharp setback during the 1997 Asian financial crisis and then a gradual slowdown to below 5%, declining further to 2%–3% after the 2008 global financial crisis. China and India, still at relatively earlier stages of development, may continue to post growth rates of 5%–7% and 6%–8%, respectively, for some time. Yet, as their income levels rise, both will inevitably face the same 'middle-income slowdown' that Japan and Korea experienced earlier.

This book measures economic growth primarily in terms of GDP.[6] Although GDP, derived from the pioneering work of *Simon Kuznets*, remains the most widely used indicator of aggregate economic performance, it is not a comprehensive measure of welfare or prosperity. Contrary to the GDP, the concept of 'Development' is multidimensional, encompassing not only income and output but also equity, poverty reduction, education, health, safety and environmental sustainability. While GDP captures the quantity of economic activity, the concept of 'Development' reflects the quality of life.

Stiglitz and his coauthors,[7] in their book *Mismeasuring Our Lives*, argued that GDP is an important but incomplete indicator of economic performance and social progress. They emphasized that GDP overlooks income distribution, environmental degradation, health, education, job security and unpaid work such as household care. They recommended complementing GDP with broader indicators that reflect inequality, environmental sustainability, social cohesion and long-term economic resilience. Their central message is that what societies choose to measure shapes policy priorities. Relying solely on GDP risks, therefore, encourages growth strategies that raise output but fail to improve overall human welfare.

Asia's rapid economic expansion has undeniably improved income and living standards, but progress in well-being has not always matched increase in income. Environmental degradation has often worsened during high-growth phases. Asia's growth miracle has carried significant environmental costs such as air and water pollution, deforestation, soil degradation and soaring greenhouse gas emissions. Although per capita emissions were once below the global average, Asia's carbon footprint has grown faster than any other region's in the 21st century. Continuing a strategy of 'grow first, clean later' is no longer viable in a world facing resource depletion and escalating climate risks.

The central policy challenge today is to redirect the focus from rapid growth toward sustainable development. Japan and Korea have already moved beyond the phase of high-speed industrial expansion, China is approaching a similar transition and India is likely to face it within the next decade. Environmental degradation and climate change have become binding constraints on future growth. The economic and social costs of more frequent floods and droughts, rising sea levels, biodiversity loss, desertification, wildfires and freshwater scarcity are global in origin but locally concentrated in their impacts. Owing to its geography, high population density and economic structure, Asia is particularly vulnerable to climate-related risks. Addressing these challenges will require not only decisive national policy responses but also stronger regional cooperation.

The green transition could represent a new frontier of economic opportunity. Global markets for renewable energy, energy efficiency and environmental goods are expanding rapidly. Asian economies already play a central role in this transformation. China and India rank among the world's largest destinations for renewable energy investment, while Asian manufacturers dominate global supply chains for solar panels, batteries and efficient lighting equipment.

6.3.2 Market plays a bigger role

During the high-growth period, the governments of the Four Asian Geese played a crucial role in driving industrialization and accelerating economic growth. They implemented targeted industrial policies, employing a wide range of measures such as tariffs, subsidies, preferential credit and tax incentives to support strategic industries. The Four Asian Tigers were not unique in adopting this approach. Most of today's advanced economies employed similar strategies during the early stages of their industrialization. However, what set the Asian economies apart was the extent and intensity of government intervention, as their governments played a more direct and comprehensive role in allocating resources and, at times, substituting for market mechanisms.

During the high-growth period, the governments of the Four Asian Geese played an active coordinating role in industrial development. By guiding investment and intervening selectively, they addressed gaps between private and social returns and steered resources toward higher value-added activities, thereby accelerating structural transformation. However, this policy approach has become less effective in an increasingly complex and technology-driven global economy. As these economies matured, the state-led strategies that had once facilitated rapid industrialization began to constrain innovation, competition and efficiency. Over time, the persistence of such policies contributed to diminishing productivity gains and slower economic growth.

In particular, the financial sector in the Four Asian Geese lagged the broader real sector, as governments maintained strong control over financial institutions and directed credit toward priority industries. During the early stages of development, when financial markets were still weak, such intervention was widely viewed as necessary to address market failures and support industrialization. As a result, the sector remained heavily regulated, and policymakers prioritized industrial expansion over the development of a modern financial system. Over time, however, this approach contributed to the underdevelopment of financial markets, leaving banks and other financial institutions lagging the real sector.

Today, many Asian economies have world-class manufacturing companies that lead in technology and market share but few globally competitive financial institutions. It is easy to name Asian global manufacturers that have become leaders in their industries. Toyota, Honda, Sony, Panasonic, Samsung, Hyundai, LG, BYD, Huawei, Lenovo, Tata and Foxconn are only a few among many world-class companies that represent Asia's industrial strength and global competitiveness. However, it is much harder to name world-class banks from the same region. Most Asian banks still depend heavily on traditional retail finance, focusing on consumer and commercial lending rather than advanced investment and global financial services. Even in Japan, a long-standing member of the G7, the financial industry's growth and international influence have remained relatively limited.

The transition from a state-led to a market-led system has been slow. The next phase of growth will depend on empowering markets to drive efficiency, innovation and competitiveness. However, this does not mean that the government should completely withdraw from economic management. Instead, its role should evolve from direct intervention to facilitation and regulation. Governments should focus on maintaining macroeconomic stability; ensuring fair competition; investing in education, research, and infrastructure; and providing social safety nets to address inequality. They must also strengthen institutions, including property rights, legal systems and corporate governance, to create an environment where markets can function effectively and equitably.

Interestingly, the US appears to be shifting in the opposite direction under President Trump's second term. Although the US has long been regarded as a strong advocate of free and open market policies, recent actions indicate a growing trend toward greater government intervention. The US government has intervened in corporate matters, such as the TikTok deal; pressured Japan, Korea and Taiwan to invest in selected strategic industries; and restricted exports of advanced technologies, including semiconductors.

At first glance, these actions might seem to represent a return to state-led industrial policy. However, the underlying reality is more complex. In the modern global economy, particularly in the field of hi-techs such as AI, the real competition is not between governments but among powerful private technology companies. The central contest is increasingly less about a direct confrontation between the US and China as nation-states and more about competition among leading technology firms. Chinese companies such as DeepSeek are emerging as competitors to major American firms, including OpenAI, Apple, Amazon and xAI.

This shift highlights the reality that the core of global technological rivalry now lies in the innovative capacity, research capabilities and scaling power of private-sector enterprises, even though state policies, regulation and industrial strategies continue to shape the competitive landscape.

6.3.3 Shared prosperity among and within countries

A serious problem facing Asia is that the benefits of growth have not been evenly shared. The widening gap between the rich and the poor, both within and among countries, has become increasingly visible. In 2017, a popular book *Crazy Rich Asians* (later made into a film) highlighted the extravagant wealth of a Singaporean family, symbolizing Asia's growing inequality. While Asia has produced many success stories, poverty persists. Of the roughly 700 million people worldwide living on less than $2.15 per day today, about 200 million reside in Asia, while the majority are now concentrated in Sub-Saharan Africa.

The relationship between economic growth and inequality has long been debated among economists and policymakers. While economic growth generally helps reduce poverty and raise income levels, it often leads to greater inequality. Particularly in recent decades, technological progress and globalization have widened wage gaps between skilled and unskilled workers. These same forces have also allowed entrepreneurs and investors to earn large profits from capital, while wages for labor have grown more slowly. Widening urban–rural divides and regional disparities have further intensified inequality.

Cases of the Four Asian Geese show mixed results in the relation between growth and inequality. In Japan, inequality initially declined during the postwar recovery and high-growth decades of the 1950s to 1970s, supported by land reforms and industrial employment. However, since the 1990s, income gaps have gradually widened due to economic stagnation, labor market dualism and population aging. In Korea, income distribution improved notably in the 1980s and 1990s but deteriorated after the Asian Financial Crisis as labor markets became more polarized. In China, *the Gini coefficient* rose sharply from below 0.31 in 1981 to 0.49 in 2008, and it has continued to increase since then, reflecting urban–rural and regional disparities. In India, inequality also worsened, with the Gini coefficient climbing from around 0.32 during 1965–1993 to 0.36 by 2011, driven by uneven regional development and structural labor shifts.

As inequality rises, public support for growth-oriented policies weakens, making it more difficult to reach consensus on economic planning and reform.[8] Widening inequality could erode social cohesion, weaken public trust and ultimately hinder growth. To avoid such risks, governments must pursue 'inclusive growth' policies. Sharing the benefits of growth fairly strengthens social cohesion, trust and collective commitment to reform. Societies with greater social capital can also respond more effectively to crises through collective action and shared purpose.

Governments vary greatly in their capacity to reduce inequality. Based on data from the early 2010s, the Gini coefficient, before taxes and transfers, was 0.400 in developing Asia and 0.468 in the European Union (EU), suggesting that Asia's pre-tax inequality was not significantly worse. After redistribution, however, the Gini coefficient fell to 0.299 in the EU but only to 0.374 in Asia. This gap shows that Asian governments have been far less effective in improving income distribution through taxation and social transfers.

Reducing income disparities is economically and politically challenging. Prime Minister *Indira Gandhi* of India, who took office in 1966, pursued policies aimed at redistributing income through tighter import controls, nationalization of banks and major industries, restrictions on large firms and rigid labor laws.[9] However, these measures slowed economic growth and, paradoxically, deepened poverty. Benevolent intentions do not always produce positive results.

Inclusive growth is an important goal for the future, but the key question is how to achieve it. First, it is essential to ensure fair competition. When competition becomes unfair or distorted, markets cannot allocate resources efficiently, and inequality tends to increase. Second, policies that promote inclusiveness must not undermine the core foundations of growth such as competition, open markets and entrepreneurship. If these principles are weakened, efforts to promote inclusion can backfire, slowing growth and ultimately widening the income gap instead of reducing it.

Income disparities across Asian countries are as significant as inequalities within individual countries. While many countries have escaped absolute poverty, development gaps remain wide in infrastructure, education, healthcare and digital access. The ADB estimates that Asia needs $1.7 trillion annually in infrastructure financing through 2030. Japan became the region's largest aid donor from the late 1970s onward.[10] Today, more Asian economies have themselves become providers of development assistance.[11] Korea,[12] Singapore, Taiwan and Hong Kong began providing official development assistance (ODA) in the late 1980s.[13] China and India have also emerged as major donors,[14] alongside ASEAN members. China's Belt and Road Initiative and the establishment of the Asian Infrastructure Investment Bank (AIIB) in 2015 have expanded infrastructure support for developing countries. India, leveraging its strengths in IT and capacity building, has provided technical assistance and humanitarian aid.

Throughout history, Asian economies have both competed and cooperated with one another. The potential gains from regional integration are immense. Closer connections through trade, investment and technological collaboration can reduce disparities and create shared prosperity. Increased trade lowers consumer prices and creates jobs. Greater investment reduces capital costs for host countries while generating returns for investors.

Finally, emerging technologies such as AI present new challenges for equity within and across economies. Those who adopt AI effectively, whether nations, firms or individuals, will capture disproportionate gains, while others risk being left behind. AI tends to concentrate data and decision-making power, potentially exacerbating inequality. Although some optimists argue that AI could eventually democratize knowledge and opportunity, this outcome depends on broad and inclusive access to benefits from AI. Technological diffusion remains uneven. Governments therefore bear a critical responsibility in designing policies that ensure fair competition, invest in human capital and expand access to digital tools so that the benefits of AI are shared equitably among people and across nations.

Notes

1 Perkins Dwight, *East Asian Development*, 2013, Harvard University Press, p153.
2 He analyzed Korea, Taiwan, Hong Kong and Sigapore.
3 Michael P. Todaro and Stephen C. Smith, *Economic Development*, 2015, Pearson, p207.
4 Michael P. Todaro and Stephen C. Smith, *Economic Development*, 2015, Pearson, p207.
5 Kolhi, Sharma, and Sood, *Asia 2050: Realizing the Asian Century*, 2011, p47.
6 It is the market value of all final goods and services produced within a country in a given year.
7 Joseph E. Stiglitz, Amartya Sen, and Jean-Paul Fitoussi.
8 Latin America's stagnation has often been attributed to deep-rooted inequality. Between 1950 and 1990, Argentina's Gini coefficient rose from 0.37 to 0.52 and Brazil's from 0.57 to 0.65.
9 The threshold of 300 in 1976 was further tightened to 100 in 1983.
10 Throughout the 1970s and 1980s, Japan achieved higher economic growth with large trade surplus and thus it could increase support for developing countries with large amount of ODAs.
11 After World War II, Asia relied heavily on external assistance, firstly from the U.S.
12 In the 1990s, Korea provided grants by the Korea International Cooperation Agency (KOICA) and concessional loans by the Economic Development Cooperation Fund (EDCF) managed by the Korea Exim bank. In 2004, Korea launched 'Korea's Knowledge Sharing Program (KSP)' to share its development experiences with developing countries. In 2009, Korea became a member of the Development Assistance Committee of the OECD, which means Korea has officially become a donor country.
13 Their early assistance focused on providing technical assistance and training as Japan did previously.
14 The Export-Import Bank of China and China Development Bank provided preferential export credits to developing buyers.

Afterword

There is a familiar saying; "If you want to fly fast, fly by yourself. But if you want to fly far, fly together with your friends". Asian countries, however, flew successfully both faster and farther. How? I think that they made it because they flew alongside neighbors, cooperating at times and competing at others. The primary objective of this book is not to explain what benefits Asian economies have exchanged among them. That is a task for a separate study. Instead, this book focused on finding the shared genes which enabled the Four Asian Geese to fly faster and farther.

I hope that the findings here can help other Asian countries who are trying to join the journey for prosperity. Upon finishing this book, some concerns, however, weighed on me heavily. Koreans refer to a golden boy or girl as 'my mother's friend's son/daughter'. That is because Korean mothers nag their children by saying "My friend's son/daughter is better than you in every aspect". Mothers expect that these words of comparison can spur their children's maximum endeavors. But, contrary to the mothers' expectations, such comparisons often discourage their children more than they motivate.

By analogy, the success story of developed countries may not give an appropriate prescription to developing countries. It does not help developing countries at all to simply say, "Be like us and you can enjoy the riches of economic growth". Economic growth is an outcome of complex interactions of many interconnected variables. One single measure cannot fix a poverty trap and accelerate economic growth. Based on a detailed diagnosis of the country, a multifaceted and practical approach can work. We acknowledge that those complicated interactions are certain to be beyond the economic analysis and policy advice which economists tend to preach. That belongs to the realm of politics and therefore to the responsibilities of political leadership.

I admit that the argument and conclusion in this book, in the aggregate, remains hypothetical because it is not verified with precise empirical data. I hope that the task of testing should be taken by subsequent research. Still, I hope that this book can provide meaningful insights which can be explored by those who work for economic development, both policymakers and economists alike. My final advice to friends in developing countries is "Don't try to copy and paste another country's policy menu. Rather, do try to design and build four pillars of your own".

For individuals, getting rich is much more important than GDP growth of his/her country. The success story of rich people may provide strong motivation and practical guidance to those who try to become rich. However, stories of the rich cannot improve the quality of life of millions and billions of people in communities and countries. This is the reason why I was eager to write this book about growth of economies. Achieving higher economic growth is the most powerful and effective way to make millions and billions of people better off and happier at once.

References

English

Daron Acemoglu, James A. Robinson, *Why Nations Fail*, Crown Business, 2012
ADB, *Asia's Journey to Prosperity*, 2020
Montek S. Ahluwalia, Economic Reforms in India since 1991: Has Gradualism Worked? *The Journal of Economic Perspectives*, 2002 16, no 3(summer 2002), 67–88
Montek S. Ahluwalia, *Backstage*, Rupa Publications India, 2020
Prasenjit K. Basu, *Asia Reborn*, Aleph Book Company, 2017
William J. Baumol, Robert E. Litan, Carl J. Schramm, *Good Capitalism, Bad Capitalism, and the Economics of Growth and Prosperity*, Yale University Press, 2007
Dick Beason, Dennis Patterson, *The Japan That Never Was*, State University of New York Press, 2004
Michael H. Best, *How Growth really Happens*, Princeton, 2018
David E. Bloom, David Canning, Jaypee Sevilla, *The Demographic Dividend*, Land, 2003
Gordon Brown, Mohamed A. El-Erian, Michael Spence, *Permacrisis, Aplan to Fix a Fractured World*, Simon & Schuster, 2023
K. C. Roy Cal Clark, *Comparing Development Patterns in Asia*, Lynne Rienner, 1997
Ha-Jon Chang, *Kicking away the Ladder*, Anthem Press, 2002
Joong-Kyung Choi, *Korea's Economic Development*, Daewon Publishing Co., 2013
Klaus Deininger, Songqing Jin, Hari K. Nagarajan, Land Reforms, Poverty Reduction, and Economic Growth: Evidence from India, Policy Research Working Paper 4448, WB
Sebastian Edwards, Latin America's decline: A long historical view, NBER Working Paper 15171, 2009
Bai Gao, *Japan's Economic Dilemma*, Cambridge University Press, 2001
Wayne Gruden, Barry Asmus, *The Poverty of Nations*, Crossway, 2013
Ashok Gulati, Shenggen Fan, *The Dragon and the Elephant*, Oxford University Press, 2007
Amitab Kant, *Made in India*, 2023, Rupa Plications Pvt. Ltd.
Robert Z. Lawrence, David E. Weinstein, Trade and Growth: Import-led or Export-led? Evidence from Japan and Korea, NBER Working Paper 7264, 1999
Takehito Nakkao, Eight Conditions for Economic Development, *Nikkei Asian Review*, Feb. 5, 2015
H. William Overholt, *The Rise of China*, W. W. Norton & Company Ltd., 1993
Arvind Panagariya, *Free Trade and Prosperity*, Oxford University Press, 2019
Jim Rohwer, *Asia Rising*, Simon & Schuster, p51, 1995

Jeffrey Sachs, *The End of Poverty*, Penguin Books, 2005
Il SaKong, Youngsun Koh, *The Korean Economy*, 2010, KDI
Michael Schuman, *The Miracle*, Happer Business, 2010
Joe Studwell, *How Asia Works*, Profile Books Limited, 2013
Dimitri Vittas, Akihiko Kawaura, Policy-based Finance, Financial regulation, and Financial Sector Development in Japan, Policy Research Working Paper 1443, The World Bank, 1995

Korean

Kyu Ha Cho, *The Japanese Economy's Economic Development Process and Causes*, Korean Economy Daily Press, 1987
Hyuk Jung, *Japan's Small but Strong Industries of Material, Parts and Equipment*, Maeil Newspaper Press, 2020
Seunghee Jwa, Changkeun Kim, *One-Night Story of Korean Economy*, Ilwoldam, 2010
Sung-jin Kang, *Theory of Economic Development*, PakYoungSa, 2018
Duk-young Kim, *East Asian Economy*, HaeNam, 2004
Kihwan Kim, *Korean Economic Miracle, 50 Years of Past and Future*, Kiparang, 2013
Chang Min Lee, *Again, Reading Japan Carefully*, The Forest, 2022
Dae geun Lee, et al., *New History of Economic Development of Korea*, Nanam Press, 2005
Enkoo Lee, *IT Revolution and India's New Birth*, Saechang Media, 2003
Shinwoo Lee, *Koreanomics*, Illi, 2013
Sihan Lee, *AI War for Hegemony*, Book Planer, 2025
Wonchul Oh, *How President Park Made Korea's Economic Success*, East West Culture, 2006
Haewon Seok, *History of Korean Economy*, Future Window, 2012

Index

Note: *Italic* page numbers refer to figures and page numbers followed by 'n' refer to notes.

For Product Safety Concerns and Information please contact our EU representative GPSR@taylorandfrancis.com Taylor & Francis Verlag GmbH, Kaufingerstraße 24, 80331 München, Germany